QUITTING

KNOWING

WHEN TO

LEAVE

DALE A. DAUTEN

Walker and Company ❊ New York, New York

TO SANDY
A "Dove Trooping with Crows"

The author is grateful to the publishers of the following books and magazine articles for permission to reprint from them in these pages. Excerpts from
On Death and Dying by Elisabeth Kübler-Ross, copyright © 1969 by Elisabeth Kübler-Ross, by permission of Macmillan Publishing Co., Inc.; *Siddhartha* by Herman Hesse, translated by Hilda Rossner, copyright © 1951 by New Directions Publishing Corporation, by permission of New Directions Publishing Corporation; *Lyndon Johnson and the American Dream* by Doris Kearns, copyright © 1976 by Doris Kearns, by permission of Harper & Row, Publishers, Inc.; *A Dangerous Place* by Daniel Patrick Moynihan, copyright © 1975, 1978 by Daniel Patrick Moynihan, by permission of Little, Brown and Company; *The Professor of Desire* by Philip Roth, copyright © 1977 by Philip Roth, by permission of Farrar, Straus & Giroux; *Dubin's Lives* by Bernard Malamud, copyright © 1977, 1979 by Bernard Malamud, by permission of Farrar, Straus & Giroux; "Less Than One" by Joseph Brodsky, reprinted with permission from *The New York Review of Books*, copyright © 1979 by Myrev, Inc.; *Blind Ambition* by John Dean, copyright © 1976 by John W. Dean, by permission of Simon & Schuster, Inc., a Division of Gulf and Western Corporation; *Second Wind: The Memoirs of an Opinionated Man* by Bill Russell and Taylor Branch, copyright © 1979 by Willian F. Russell, by permission of Random House, Inc.; *The Centaur* by John Updike, copyright © 1963 by John Updike, by permission of Alfred A. Knopf; *Illusions* by Richard Bach, copyright © 1977 by Creature Enterprises, Inc., by permission of Delacorte Press; *My Life in the Mafia* by Vincent C. Teresa and Thomas C. Renner, copyright © 1973 by Vincent Charles Teresa and Thomas C. Renner, by permission of Doubleday and Company, Inc.; *Marjoe* by Steven Gaines, copyright © 1973 by Marjoe Gortner and Steven S. Gaines, by permission of Harper & Row, Publishers, Inc.; *Once to Every Man* by William Sloane Coffin, copyright © 1977 by William Sloane Coffin, Jr., by permission of Atheneum Publishers; *Decision Making* by Irving L. Janis and Leon Mann, copyright © 1977 by the Free Press, a division of Macmillan Publishing Co., Inc.

First published in the United States of America in 1980 by the Walker Publishing Company, Inc.

Published simultaneously in Canada by Beaverbooks, Limited, Don Mills, Ontario.

ISBN: 0-8027-0660-6

Library of Congress Catalog Card Number: 80-51337

Printed in the United States of America

Book designed by Robert Barto

10 9 8 7 6 5 4 3 2 1

CONTENTS

ACKNOWLEDGMENTS

There are three groups of individuals who helped with this book.

I am indebted to all those quitters and stayers who agreed to be interviewed and who allowed me to chronicle their heroics of everyday life.

Several people assisted me with the mechanics of interviewing and drafting. My thanks to Ken Hollander, Mary Ben-eliezer, Barb Rosenberg, David Feldman, Bruce Brittain, Suzanne Berk, Donna Galway, Kathy Mayfield, and especially, Shari Butler.

Finally, I am grateful to Sam Walker and his associates—in particular, Ruth Cavin—for their willingness to work with a new author on an unusual, some would say risky, subject. Ruth was the doctor who presided at the birth of this book and I especially thank her for her dedication to excellence, her willingness to ask hard questions, and her friendship.

I knew that suffering did not
ennoble; it degraded. It made
men selfish, mean, petty, and
suspicious. It absorbed them
in small things. It did not
make them more than men; it
made them less than men.

W. Somerset Maugham
The Summing Up

PREFACE

THERE was a touching naïveté to my early lovemaking that, in recollection, still brings a silly grin to my face. My first sexual intercourse occurred, incredibly, by accident. We were two teen-age Baptists who were determined to save ourselves for marriage, but who nonetheless had indulged in spending the night together in a mountain "resort motel." As we lay there, I in my underwear, she in a nightgown, our bodies somehow managed to unite sexually despite our clothes. We took this small miracle as a signal of divine approval.

What most characterized our continuing relations was laughter and playfulness; the children had discovered the adult secret. Then into our Eden came the knowledge of right and wrong—not the morality of the deed (we had rationalized that successfully), but the correctness or incorrectness of Technique. As sex manuals became available to me, I became more serious with sex, enjoyed it less, did it less. Years were spent unlearning the lessons of "correctness."

I tell this little story to explain how I came to have an aversion to "how to" manuals for anything more human than fixing the sink. Although I have an almost reverent fondness for the printed word, I am suspicious of books that offer paternal counsel on how to live. True, the book you hold is my attempt to explain how knowing when to end relationships is important to a fulfilled, happy life. I will try to offer the insights two years of research provided. But as Jack Webb used to say on the old *Dragnet* show, "Just the facts, ma'am. Just the facts." I have tried to argue my case well, and I hope this book may even help some who read it, but I have tried always to remember "the facts."

The facts to be presented are the result of extensive research on how and why individuals leave important relationships—a job, a marriage, a friendship, whatever; how and why people quit.

The research started with the observation that even in the most obviously failed relationships—say, a disastrous career or a destructive marriage—many of the "victims" refused to quit. Some went so far as to take pride in their refusal. Questions: Is quitting so very dangerous? If not, why is it so feared? Can we pinpoint the circumstances when quitting would be most appropriate? Can the probable outcome of a decision to quit be predicted? These questions warranted serious answers.

In 1978 and 1979 I discussed nearly two hundred quitting situations with 120 individuals who had lived through them (many people had faced two or more different quitting situations). The majority of the cases (125 of 195) involved making a decision to quit an important relationship—usually a career change or a divorce, although abortions, a sex change, leaving family members, or other special situations were encountered. The remaining cases were those where a decision to quit was considered but the individual decided *not* to leave. Whether the person was a quitter or a stayer, the outcome of his or her decision was scored on its "success" by examining three factors: how quickly and thoroughly the person accepted and adjusted to the decision; how frequent and severe were any regrets; and how likely the individual would be to repeat the same decision.* In

---

*I have been questioned about the "morality" of the "success" criterion: Isn't there a higher good than happiness or lack of regret? This question reminds me of one Woody Allen asks and answers in Getting Even: "Can we actually 'know' the universe? My God, it's hard enough finding your way around in Chinatown." The criterion of "success" utilizes happiness and absence of regret as its measure, making the "morality" of the decision the individual's—each person's morality should be reflected in the extent of his or her own regret or happiness.

addition, a number of elements that were part of the decision were also scored—subjective components such as the "selfishness" of the decision, as well as more objective criteria such as "time between the decision to quit and the actual departure." By measuring as many aspects of the quitting decision as possible, I was able to analyze the factors that lead to successful quitting.

One important early finding of the research was that major quitting decisions, whether they lead to a career change, a divorce, or some other particular action, have the same underlying factors. Because all important quitting situations involve the same fundamental human dynamics, they can be analyzed together. Therefore, career cases, marital cases, and others are interwoven throughout this book.

Those are the background facts about research in a difficult and largely unexplored area. The remainder of this book is devoted to the *results*: a surprising and, I believe, useful set of facts.

I

INTRODUCTION—

AN OVERVIEW

(THE PLAYERS: A seventy-one-year old woman and her granddaughter. The scene: Driving grandmother to her retirement party, the evening after her last day at a job held for forty-three years.)

Granddaughter: To stay at one job for forty-three years . . . you must have really loved your work.

Grandmother: No. Mostly I hated it.

Granddaughter: Hated it? Why would you stay if you hated it?

Grandmother: Because I never quit.

Granddaughter: If you hated it, why didn't you quit?

Grandmother: Sometimes I was too busy. Sometimes I was too scared.

A true story. And, other than the extreme length of time involved, a familiar story.

Regrets. Peek into a failed relationship, behind the forced cheerfulness and the learned optimism, and find . . . regrets:

I've been a paper salesman for seven years. I never could stand it. I hate to get up in the morning. They've sent me to those inspiration seminars and tried to teach me how to

[5]

convince myself that I love what I'm doing, but the only way I get through the day is to spend my lunch parked by the lake smoking dope.

*   *   *

I was married for seven years. Every day for seven years I trudged down to the tracks and lay down. Sure enough, every day the train ran over me. One day I didn't show up. One day I finally caught on and walked the other way. I wasted seven years learning how to walk away.

*   *   *

Since the early days of my sexual awakening, I knew I was gay. I tried for years and years to be straight, too ignorant to admit what I wanted and needed. I ran over a lot of people trying to run from myself.

This research began with the observation that individuals in wrecked relationships often choose to carry on, languishing in a prison with unlocked doors, too proud or determined or scared or lazy or ignorant to quit. Why are people so afraid to quit? Because of the danger of regret? In the cases studied, both quitters and nonquitters had regrets—but the regret in the two groups was of a profoundly different nature: Of those people interviewed who quit, *most regretted not having quit sooner*; of the cases where the individual considered quitting but decided *not* to quit, *most regretted their decision to stay.*

Is quitting risky? Yes—about one-quarter of those who quit made a mistake. But quitting is far less dangerous than not quitting; when faced with an unsatisfactory relationship, over half of the nonquitters made a mistake. Thus, regret was more than twice as likely among nonquitters.

Naturally, never to have to face an unsatisfactory relationship, and thus never to face a decision to quit, would be ideal. But of those who were confronted with an unsatisfactory relationship, the ones who quit were more successful than the ones who stayed. Action leads to success more often than inaction does.

Quitting works. Quitting works better than not quitting. So, the odds favor the quitter . . . usually. But who is usual? One person, alone and vulnerable, must decide to quit. Quitting remains difficult, frightening. Even among those who were "successful quitters," an average of five years elapsed from the time the relationship turned unsatisfactory to the time of the actual quit, an average of five years spent in unhappiness and indecision. For those who did not quit, the indecision often continues . . . five years, twenty years, a lifetime. Why?

THE PARADOXES OF INACTION

What is the world's greatest force for progress?
Hope.
What is the single greatest deterrent to positive change?
Hope.

The first of the three great paradoxes of inaction involves hope: Hope can pull a life forward or can sit a life down and say, Wait. Hope is often typecast as a heroine: A singer about to give up his music suddenly gets new hope and tries again, or an aging scientist tries yet another experiment to discover the cure to what has been an incurable disease. Both, of course, succeed. In this book, about what people do when they find themselves in unsatisfactory relationships, Hope will be a villain. She deserves it; of the 125 quitting stories derived from the interviews on which this book is based, Hope and her companions were responsible for a total of about five hundred years of unhappiness. In these stories the princess did not kiss the toad, the glass slipper never fit—yet the toads and washerwomen waited and hoped. Five hundred years wasted . . . waiting, hoping.

When a person is drowning in a career or a marriage, hope comes, but not to the rescue. Hope provides more breath, one breath at a time: "It will work out." "This too, shall pass." The person stays afloat but remains lost at sea. Hope prevents a resolution, forestalls the end, forestalls change or action.

One of the surprises of this research is how vital a role *hopelessness* plays in bringing about constructive change.

What causes people to stay in unhappy relationships?
The fear of unhappiness.

Individuals fear becoming what they already are. When individuals are in unhealthy relationships, they frequently respond not by running for freedom but by fearing freedom. Having

made a mistake by entering into the relationship, they have
learned to be afraid of mistakes. They have also learned to mistrust their own judgment, the judgment that brought them into
the relationship. When that same judgment starts to tell them
the relationship is not working, they are skeptical, not certain
that another reverse will not occur. If they once wanted that
marriage or career, maybe they will want it again. So they conclude: There is no certainty. This conclusion forgets a critical
reality, a critical certainty: The relationship has caused and is
still causing unhappiness. The palliative of hope is less intimidating than change.

Together, hope and fear combine to deny a vision of a better
future. Hope offers some wan possibility of improvement without change; fear denies the possibility of positive action.

What is the greatest rationale for selfish behavior?
Unselfishness.

The third of the paradoxes of inaction involves selfishness.
Unselfishness is the perfect excuse for inaction—no need to
admit to fear, no need to give up hope. Inaction is made heroic.
The unlucky hero saves an unhappy relationship.

There is another, broader paradox of inaction that helps explain the ironic triplets, hope, happiness, and unselfishness:
Quitting is action, but even in a society that worships action,
quitting, like retreat, is devalued, even despised.

Quitting is not only action, it is discontent become deed. Still,
quitting is not admired as other actions are. Quitting is often an
admission that a person made a mistake, chose the wrong path.
Just as often, quitting is a statement that it would be a mistake to
stay longer—a preferable path is chosen. Rather than being accepted as an admission of error or of potential error, quitting is
often misconstrued to be the error itself. Quitting *can* be a mistake, but more often it is the resolution or redressing of a mistake. Nonetheless, the word *quitter* has the same dark connotations as *mistake, failure, surrender,* and *desertion.* Action is admired,
but less so than success—better the illusion of success than the
admission of failure and the act of quitting.

If quitting were simply weak like, say, surrender or retreat, to quit would merely be an embarrassment; unfortunately, the animus against quitting is deeper and less easily forgotten. A pervasive, if inchoate, part of the conventional wisdom is the belief that a person should be capable of rising above circumstance. A theme of virtually every important philosophical current in the mainstream of American culture is the assertion that an individual's environment or resources (personal or material) should not matter, do not matter—that with enough effort an individual can overcome any situation, rise above it, transcend it. This is, of course, as much lie as truth—a half-truth so familiar that it passes across the borders of logic with a nod of recognition rather than a suspicious search of its baggage.

A brief summary shows that the wisdom of America counsels transcendence—the myth that "circumstances do not matter."

Christianity

The New Testament declares the day of judgment near; there is no time for ordinary happiness, only for spiritual purification. From this assumption flow a number of conclusions about daily life: "Having food and raiment, let us be content." "Love your enemies." "Turn the other cheek." In Christianity each individual's situation is simply his obstacle to salvation, and all eyes should be fixed on the next life.

Inspiration/Motivation

An important contributor to the *Zeitgeist* is the Norman Vincent Peale, Dale Carnegie, "dare to be great," "think and grow rich" school of Protestant-oriented success motivation. This familiar philosophy says PMA (Positive Mental Attitude) is the key to wealth, popularity, whatever the head or other parts of the body desire. For example, the latest success at selling success, Zig Ziglar, former cookware salesman and now the nation's most popular motivational speaker, receives up to $2,500 an appearance to tell audiences, "All of you are destined for accomplishment, engineered for success, endowed with the seeds of greatness," and to give homework assignments such as his "Dream Sheet" (instructions: "List some of the things you want—the beautiful home, the trip around the world, the brand-new automobile"). Attitudes, not circumstances, matter.

Existentialism

Although most existentialists find the concept of material success nonsensical, they, too, believe in transcending one's situation. A part of the transcendence is simply uninterest—life is absurd, meaningless, so why be overly concerned with the world? Even poor, mythical Sisyphus should be stronger than his position. "There is no fate that cannot be surmounted by scorn," says Camus of Sisyphus. "The struggle itself toward the heights is enough to fill a man's heart. One must imagine Sisyphus happy." Even the most pathetic, hopeless circumstances can be surmounted.

Orientalism

Traditional Orientalism, particularly Buddhism, has the goal of detachment ("nonattachment" in the newer jargon). The object is *not* to discover the self but to lose the self in search of a higher reality. Day to day reality is illusion.

D. T. Suzuki, describing Buddhism, says,

> The reason we are so annoyed in our daily life, and unable to escape from its annoyance, is due to our intellectual inability to go beyond the intellect. . . . We must admit that all the vexations and anxieties of life are due to our failure to sink into our own centre.

Neo-Orientalism

Take Oriental philosophy, forget its redoubtable discipline (mental and physical), alter its purpose (from denying the self to finding the self)—in other words, disembowel it but give it a suntan—and, presto, you have Ameri-Zen, the spindly, Occidental cousin of Zen. Ameri-Zen is the New Orientalism, an attempt to steal the insights but not the rigors of Zen and Buddhism, an attempt to arrive without a journey. Although the discipline may be forgotten, the promise is the same—an ability to deny the power of circumstances. In the words of Paul Williams, "Each of us is responsible for every aspect of his creation." If we are ill, we choose to be ill. If a career is failing, we wanted it to fail. We choose every aspect of our creation. Reality is relative, so we choose our own reality.

Some basic tenets of a popular, accepted, and acceptable philosophy are "hope for all," "a better world," "each person already holds the key," "believing is becoming," "reality is adjustable," "change your attitude and change the world." Failure and defeat are simply wished away. The familiar conclusion is reached: Circumstances do not matter. Truth enough to be believable. Believable enough to be dangerous. Dangerous enough to leave millions trapped in unfulfilling, even destructive relationships—millions who refuse to fail, and in doing so imprison themselves in failure. Camus tells us we must picture Sisyphus happy. The modern Sisyphus, condemned to toil at the hopeless labor of changing reality without changing environments, we must picture as smiling through his tears, telling himself that he is happy, knowing it is not true.

But the modern Sisyphus is condemned to his labor only by his perceptions. The final paradox is that an individual who has failed to alter a relationship satisfactorily by dint of willpower must give up believing that he can alter his circumstances through transcendence. He must physically alter his environment: Only by admitting that his current philosophy is ineffectual can he become effective.

OBSTACLES TO ACTION

Although the paradoxes of inaction may be overcome and the philosophical objections to quitting dismissed, a number of *practical* obstacles remain. The fear of quitting important relationships is not simply mistaken philosophy, it is a recognition of the burdens the quitter assumes:

> No matter who *drives* whom to quit, the one who quits a relationship "officially" ends it and is often considered the initiator, receiving the greater proportion of blame. The co-workers or loved ones left behind are given permission to be martyrs. These survivors involve others in speculation about the cause of their "desertion." (To have been "deserted" may even provide the abandoned party with a superior legal position in property disputes.)

Although the person who quits may have recognized that the philosophy and practice of transcendence is a failure, smug believers in transcendence will continue to label one who leaves a "quitter," and as any high school football coach knows, "Winners never quit; quitters never win." Quitting carries a stigma.

Even if a relationship is basically untenable, it is rarely completely unsatisfactory. A hopeless career has some rewards (most often some friendships) and inspires some psychological or physical dependence; this is true also of a marriage, a city, or a family.

The good must be abandoned with the bad, and ambivalence is usually the most prevalent state of mind a quitter should expect in the weeks preceding and following departure. Quitting creates a hole in a person's life. At the time, that hole is a void, an unknown. Only later will it usually be recognized as a doorway to improved circumstances.

THE PREDICTABILITY OF SUCCESS

Given the philosophical and physical impediments to quitting, the tendency to remain in a relationship past the point where it has failed is understandable; the tendency to wait for a relationship to turn so destructive that it disintegrates rather than face all the uncertainties of quitting is logical. However, the principal uncertainty, the likely "success" of quitting, *can be foretold*. The outcome of a decision to quit can be successfully predicted.

Predicting success in quitting is possible by analyzing the various components of the decision to quit and of the act of quitting itself. The cases of quitting studied were dissected, and each element of the situation was analyzed and scored. The relationship between the success of the quit and each element of the quit was then determined.*

A list of twelve elements of quitting was developed. The twelve were then analyzed for their usefulness in explaining success.

The analysis utilized the statistical techniques of correlations and multiple-regression analysis.

Four of the elements are closely related to success and together can reliably predict the success of a quit. Those four success components are

1. Realization of failure—the extent to which a sudden, dramatic recognition of defeat occurred

2. Awareness of the future—the frequency of envisioning the future of the relationship and its importance to the decision

3. "Selfishness"—the magnitude and intensity with which self-interest was applied, as opposed to "unselfish" criteria

4. "Cleanness" of the decision—the extent to which the decision could be characterized as a sudden, overwhelming sense of certainty.

A strong realization of failure makes a successful quit more likely, as do a vivid awareness of the future, a sense of selfishness, and a quality of cleanness to the decision. And when all four components are strong and clear, success is virtually certain.

SUCCESS COMPONENTS ONE AND TWO: THE FUTURE AND THE REALIZATION OF FAILURE

The first great secret of successful quitting is hopelessness. Hopelessness is the deflowered goddess of quitters. Hopelessness is a statement of the present *and of the future* (and is therefore a component of success), it goes, this relationship is unsatisfactory *and will remain* unsatisfactory; there is no light at the end of the tunnel, for the tunnel never ends. No more waiting for change. Take it or leave it. Crossing the Rubicon from hope to hopelessness is acknowledging a highly likely future, the No Change or the Change for the Worse. The component of successful quitting that measured the quitters' awareness of the future was closely related to success because it measured how important the "future not chosen" was to the quitting decision.*

A cold look at a dark future is the common impetus to a dramatic *realization of failure* (the second component of success). True hopelessness requires more than just a sense that a relationship is stagnant or in decline. Certainty that the relationship *cannot be saved* is also needed. The histories of those who were successful in their quitting usually included a sudden acknowledgment of defeat. The individual had previously acknowledged and had endeavored to ameliorate the relationship's shortcomings when the realization hit that not only had the salvage efforts failed but all other efforts were also doomed to fail. True hopelessness demands impotence with legs: Circumstances *do* matter, and the individual accepts his inability to alter or rise above the situation except by walking away.

Given the prevalence of the transcendence myth, the admission of impotence does not come readily. The bubble of hope has a thick skin; it takes a hammer and nail, not a pinprick, to

---

*This attempt to envision the future is not at all like daydreaming about how life might be better—about a different career or a different spouse—such is the behavior of the person who still hopes. The Hopeless Man's focus is on his unsatisfactory relationship. The hopelessness that makes one decide to quit is not a relative feeling—the current relationship as compared with other possible relationships. That leads to doubt and regret. True hopelessness is specific and individual. A relationship must be abandoned because of its own weaknesses rather than its relative weaknesses. If, when isolated, a relationship is undesirable, the inevitable setbacks in new postquitting relationships will not be seen as an indictment of the decision to quit.

An example will make this clear. Mr. Barr is currently a lawyer who has doubts about staying in the practice of law. If he carefully examines his future in law and decides it is not a future he wants to live, he can quit with little fear of regret (assuming that the other components of success also point to quitting). Even when his new career falters, he can be glad to have left law. If, however, Barr had begun to daydream about a future as, say, an architect and had quit law to pursue that dream, should his reality as an architect not live up to his idealized vision (a likely occurrence), his reaction would be to think of his law career, to wonder and perhaps to regret. The Hopeless Man quits a career because he recognized the shortcomings of that career. If the new career fails, he will logically move on to a third career rather than back to the first. The Hopeless Man knows what he left and why. The Hopeful Man, the dreamer, chases a new dream; if the new pursuit does not match the dream, he is vulnerable to feelings of remorse.

burst it. The unwelcome vision of defeat was usually the result of some event—for example, a wedding anniversary or a missed job promotion. The event may or may not seem significant to the objective observer, but the impact on the potential quitter is unforgettable. The abrupt insight that one is impotent and thus hopeless is a transformation that turns a life around, sending the Hopeless Person running down a mountain he or she may have spent years climbing.

SUCCESS COMPONENT THREE: SELFISHNESS

Elisabeth Kübler-Ross, in her famous report *On Death and Dying*, says that hope is, literally, life:

> If a patient stops expressing hope, it is usually a sign of imminent death. They may say, "Doctor, I think I have had it," or "I guess this is it," or they may put it like the patient who always believed in a miracle, that one day greeted us with the words, "I think this is the miracle—I am ready now and not even afraid anymore." All these patients died within twenty-four hours.

Relationships do not die so easily. Years, even half a lifetime, may pass between the acceptance of hopelessness and the end of the relationship. With the end of hope comes the death of the relationship. Although the hopeless individual may continue the association, the relationship is never the same. It is dead in spirit, if not in body. Nonetheless, the individual remains, does not quit completely, does not find success. Before the person quits, the last of the paradoxes of inaction must be encountered and overcome, and the practical obstacles to quitting must be surmounted.

The three paradoxes of inaction are hope, happiness, and unselfishness, all part of the larger paradox of action without acts, transcendence. Hopelessness of course opposes hope, vanquishes the fear of unhappiness by making clear the future of the relationship, and makes transcendence absurd. But hopelessness cannot cope with *unselfishness* (selfishness is the third component of success). The individual who attempts to remain in a hopeless situation is imposing a will that arises from outside of the unsatisfactory relationship. The decision is no longer objective. A moral judgment is made, or so it seems. Unselfishness is often the grand rationale for the pursuit of self-interest and is often used as psychological permission to act in a desired manner. That others may be helped or hurt is irrelevant: Selfishness is labeled "unselfishness." However, unselfishness is not always so artful and may in fact be a choice of another person's interest over one's own. Sadly, such an act of altruism rarely succeeds. Those who chose unselfishness nearly always regretted and often reversed their decision. If an individual has determined that a relationship is and will be unsatisfactory—that is, has achieved hopelessness—yet decides to remain for the sake of partners, spouse, children, or other loved ones, the very act of choosing unselfishness makes the relationship even less bearable. The nonquitter knows his sacrifice; it is a tiresome burden and one without end. The individual receives no reward for the sacrifice except the continuation of that which he does not desire. The relationship tends to deteriorate. Over time the nonquitter finds the beneficiaries of this act less and less worthy of it. Often they will eventually be seen as unworthy, and the individual will ultimately quit. The person who succeeds in remaining unselfish and does not quit is likely to have many regrets, frequently questioning his decision.

SUCCESS COMPONENT FOUR: THE CLEAN DECISION

By the time a person has seen the future, realized hopelessness, and asserted self-interest, that person has in effect decided that he *wants* to quit. There is a commitment to desire, but not necessarily to action. The person may also want to be younger, taller, richer; wanting and proceeding have not necessarily merged into determination. The objective obstacles to quitting—property concerns, legal matters, the stigma, the physical and psychological dislocation—come to the fore once the desire to quit is acknowledged. In successful quits, there usually occurred at this point a magic moment of decision, the *clean quitting decision* (the final component of success). The experience of a clean decision appears to be as much a subconscious resolution as an act of conscious will to reach the decision. The clean decision is a dramatic realization of victory, akin to the dramatic realization of failure. The individual abruptly knows clearly and intensely that he will quit. Often this decision is heralded by physical reactions. Herman Hesse poetically describes in *Siddhartha* the physical responses that accompanied his character's great decisions:

> Siddhartha stood still and for a moment an icy chill stole over him. He shivered inwardly like a small animal, like a bird or a hare.

and later:

> Siddhartha looked up and around him, a smile crept over his face, and a strong feeling of awakening from a long dream spread right through his being. Immediately he walked again, quickly, like the man who knows what he has to do.

Intimidating obstacles are pushed aside. The more strongly the individual realizes defeat, senses the unacceptability of the future, and asserts self interest, the greater the momentum toward the quitting decision; the cleaner the resultant decision, the greater the momentum toward actually overcoming inaction and carrying out the quit. In all the research, a vivid and palpable presence of all four major components was always associated with a successful quit.

SEEING THE

DARKNESS—THE

REALIZATION

Descartes's famous *cogito ergo som*—his "I think, therefore I am" —is a rare victory in the struggle to separate reality from illusion. Human relationships are, of course, an inseparable blend of the two. The bond that unites two people in one endeavor is so thorough a mix of attitudes, perceptions, expectations, and myths that "reality" loses any connotation as concrete or absolute. There is no standard by which to judge a relationship except the satisfaction of those involved. Following Descartes, a person examining a relationship could conclude, "I think I'm happy, therefore I am." Unfortunately, the inverse is equally true, and when people realize they are unhappy they surely are. This chapter is the story of how and why a person acknowledges unhappiness.

Thinking of all the failing relationships one sees and all the collateral open complaining one hears, unhappiness is clearly a simple matter. Still, admitting that an important relationship is and will be unhappy is often quite difficult, for doing so is to admit to having failed in at least one key area of one's life— having failed to transcend circumstances.

In explaining how a culture tends to observe changes in itself, Marshall McLuhan said that society was like the driver of a car who never saw what was ahead or alongside but looked only in the rearview mirror. This "rearview mirror effect" is true of a relationship as well—it fails long before one or more of the parties to it actually recognize the failure. Furthermore, the tendency of those in a failed relationship is to look away in order to avoid acknowledging failure.

Although illusion and self-deception are a part of all relationships, individuals who are committed to a relationship that is not working typically indulge in layers of rationalization atop the ordinary myths. They hope to insulate it from the possibility of "failure." Such relationships have already failed (in the sense of not having given the individuals what they sought), but normally, a relationship is not declared a failure until somebody quits.

Important relationships, because of their nature, are difficult to declare a failure and difficult to leave. Instead, when problems are recognized, individuals are told (usually by themselves) that "It's a phase," "Things will work out," or "It happens to everybody." Even in the most destructive situations, these "It'll be okay" myths are capable of sustaining a relationship for months, years, sometimes lifetimes. These myths are the stuff of hope, and hope—though it fortunately doesn't always spring eternal—can certainly be a cloying companion. Indeed, "not giving up hope" is itself the substance of a load of society's advice; it implicitly encourages individuals to live with failure rather than admit to having failed and, by doing so, begin to redress the failure.

Descartes speaks of the pain and fear in actually confronting reality; that is, in giving up a dream. The captive in his metaphor could be a person trapped in a failed relationship; the dream of liberty, the hope for change:

> And just as a captive who in sleep enjoys an imaginary liberty, when he begins to suspect that his liberty is but a dream, fears to awaken, and conspires with these agreeable illusions that the deception may be prolonged, so insensibly of my own accord that I fall back into my former opinions that life is as it seems, and I dread awakening from this slumber, lest the laborious wakefulness which would follow the tranquility of this repose should

have to be spent not in daylight, but in the excessive darkness of the difficulties [of a different reality].

It is worth repeating that the fear of quitting is rational: An individual who leaves a relationship must bear the stigma of "quitter"; the one who quits must shoulder the responsibility for ending the relationship; and the parties involved must give up a great deal of the dependence that is in and on any important relationship. So it is logical to avoid the Realization, the dramatic recognition of defeat. However, as the following cases illustrate, the Realization can be a strong impetus to positive change: It is both the end and the beginning.

SEEING THE DARKNESS

Everyone has a friend who is openly miserable in his or her marriage, a friend who finds fault in each detail of his or her spouse and retreats to a well-fortified position to avoid real human contact with the husband or wife.

Viola Kerns was once one of these people. She was unhappily married for thirty-one years. When asked when she first realized that her marriage was not going to work, she said with certainty that she had determined that she and Edward were not compatible at least eight weeks before the wedding. As proof of that conviction she unpacked a box of love, hate, and indifference letters and produced a "Dear John" letter written to her fiancé a month before the wedding. In it she stated, clearly and convincingly, why they were incompatible.

Why had she married a few weeks after making a *prima facie* case against the marriage? Viola said that she had failed her chemistry midterm and wanted out of college. She wanted to hurt her parents for forcing her to go to a college that would keep her away from the older Italian man she had fallen for the previous year. She, of course, could not have guessed that she was trading a bad semester of college and some small revenge for thirty-one bad years of marriage. She simply assured herself it would work out.

Did it work out? Viola felt, during all thirty-one years of her married life, that she had made a mistake. Why didn't she end the marriage sooner? She explained,

> Both of us were very responsible people. We had a very polite marriage. I suppose that was one of the major things wrong: We came from backgrounds where marriage was supposed to be a sacrifice. Responsibilities always came first. And when you take care of responsibilities first, there is no second—there's no time left. Both of us settled down to become responsible people and nothing more.
>
> If I started to suspect that the relationship was not all I wanted, I would just concentrate on something else . . . children, house, neighbors. Sometimes I felt like I was a lovely birthday present I wanted to give to my husband. But how come he didn't want to take it?
>
> Well, I'd think about a new couch, or about toilet training—toilet training became an important part of my life—or even about my husband's retirement. At twenty-five I was worried about his retirement. This trivia would drive the doubt away.

And this sustained you for thirty years?

> Yes and no. By themselves, those thoughts sustained me for eight years. After about eight years, we discovered tranquilizers. Yeah, I really bought it. I went to our kindly family doctor very upset: "I have everything in the world to be happy about. Why am I not?" I was told in a very nice way that I was different; I was a thoroughbred, and thoroughbreds are high-strung.

In this fashion Viola tried out various myths, discarding them as they wore out. Viola was not sufficiently experienced with relationships to be certain whether she was happy. Because happiness is difficult to measure, she applied the more concrete yardstick of material success to her marriage and, forcing a smile, announced to the world that she was a success. Yet she never really believed her own measurement. She asked for help—from friends, the family doctor, the minister—and all were reassuring: It would work out. In fact, Viola would still be married had not a relentless string of major incidents forced her to a Realization.

Viola's first glimpses of reality came indirectly, through an emotionally handicapped child. During six years of her son's psychoanalysis, Viola was to discover slowly that she and her son had the same problem. One patient and his mother became two patients.

Unlike other major sources of current cultural wisdom, the practical wisdom of psychoanalysis concentrates on examining oneself, emphasizing feelings. This emphasis can greatly damage the illusions that hold relationships together. Yet psychoanalysis has not been a panacea for failed relationships, and Viola's case is no anomaly: Psychoanalysis and its teachings often merely add a new source of internal turmoil to already difficult life decisions. While psychoanalytic thinking has made people more aware of their discontent, the old myths have survived, reinforced by new versions of the same stories.

The most common philosophical undercurrent of recent psychoanalytic thinking is Zen. The new version of the old lie that circumstances do not and should not matter is that individuals should rise above their environment, finding strength and peace in meditation, ultimately in Nirvana. Nirvana is an interesting concept, for it asserts that happiness is found in perfect nothingness. (The Sanskrit root word *nirva* means "to be extinguished.") The soul of Zen is to experience the Void. The effect of Zen, particularly Ameri-Zen, the third- to thirtieth-hand version of Zen now widely disseminated, is that individuals should be able to overcome the "mere" existence that surrounds them. Peace is possible in the midst of the most abject existence—and since no American qualifies as having a truly abject existence, one ought to be able to find peace despite one's circumstances.

Thus an old myth like "Things will work out; they always do" is replaced by a more glib, new myth like "Things have already worked out; you have yet to realize it." Neither conviction is conducive to constructive change.

Overall, then, while psychoanalytic thinking is encouraging an encounter with feelings (and particularly with dissatisfactions), its philosphical running mate, Zen, is encouraging Nothingness.

Viola was caught in this feeling-inaction trap. With analysis she began discovering herself—an act that consisted mostly of putting her unhappy feelings into words. She turned inward, seeking happiness in private pursuits, including the very private ones of self-observation, self-reflection, and self-analysis. In Viola's words,

> The more I got in touch with who I was and what I wanted, the farther apart we drifted. I just got more and more into me. The more I got into me, the more I would start to express it—mostly psychology bullshit. But it had become a very important part of my life, and I was un-raveling my own mysteries. It was a journey, a quest.

Viola believed that analysis would result in the contented marriage that had eluded her for twenty-five years. She spent three years in search of herself; once she found herself, she felt, the marriage would right itself.

However, while Viola was taking her inner journeys, her husband, Edward, was taking a number of extended business trips to Dallas, where he had found a woman interested in his problems and needs. The discovery of his infidelity was another encounter with the reality of their unsuccessful marriage:

> After months of wondering what in the hell was the matter with this man, on September 30, our anniversary, we were sitting in the living room. He told me he had something to tell me that he just couldn't contain anymore. He had met somebody in Dallas that he really felt close to and was really torn apart by it. This is a very honorable man, with very high moral standards for himself. He was feeling very guilty and very uncomfortable at the thought that he, a married man with a family, could have feelings for or be attracted to someone else. I had two reactions when I heard that. One reaction was anger, because this was something I had asked for repeatedly and wanted

greatly—the intimacy and closeness. The other was disbelief—what timing, what incredible timing! Our anniversary! My God!

I was far enough into psychology and all the other stuff to come up with all the absolutely ridiculous statements like, "I'm really glad you had an opportunity to experience something like that," when really if I had gone along with my inner, gut feelings, I would have taken the ashtray, smashed it over his head and called him a lousy son of a bitch. But there was no way—we had a very civilized, respectful marriage. I was trying to be very understanding. I think the shock wore off somewhere down the road.

That evening we decided that something was not right with our marriage.

For twenty-nine years Viola had been critical of her husband and her marriage, but only after Edward confessed to an affair did she recognize the possibility that the relationship might end. Predictably, this brush with the obvious frightened both Edward and Viola. They made an appointment with a marriage counselor the day after Edward's confession. Both vowed to start anew.

Kenneth Boulding, economist and social scientist, has spoken of "the law of contrary consequences," his assertion that most organized efforts at change ultimately result in the *unintended* effects being far more important than the *intended* effects. (An example Boulding uses is the social and economic discipline imposed on Japan and West Germany after World War II, which resulted in those two countries having the healthiest economies in the world, far healthier than those of the Allied nations that imposed the discipline.)

Marriage counseling—like its parent, psychoanalysis—often exemplifies this "law of contrary consequences." Far more successful at identifying problems than at solving them, counseling often has the net effect of driving marriage partners farther apart. This was true of Viola and Edward; each counseling session was supposed to help salvage their marriage, but instead each session was a realization of the fruitlessness of their relationship.

Still, Viola was a patient and very determined woman. She refused to give up. Roughly a year following the confession of his protracted affair with a woman in Dallas, Edward's company "insisted" he return to Dallas for an extended business trip.

Thirty years in an unhappy marriage and a year of marriage counseling had prepared Viola for some experimentation. Shortly after Edward departed for Dallas, Viola persuaded a single woman friend to go drinking with her. They discussed "the single life" for hours. Then Viola gave it a try: She struck up a conversation with a man who was sitting alone. Within four hours they had dined, ditched the single friend, danced, and had passionate sex.

Viola continued her affair for eight months. Although she claims to be conscious of it only in retrospect, she began to leave clues for Edward, who had returned (and had pronounced that he was faithful while in Dallas). He finally confronted her with the evidence. She describes her reaction:

> I remember my exact words—which at best were cruel, but they were a carry-over from when I had really wanted to hit him over the head with the ashtray. I said, "Yes, I met someone who fucked my brains out."
>
> In my own crazy way, I felt like that erased everything. He made his mistake, and I went and soothed my hurt vanity, and we could then throw all the garbage out the window, close the chapter, and get down to really being with each other.

But Edward was not so quick to declare the score even, the chapter closed. Before the evening ended, they had a shouting match, tossed drinks at each other; Edward threw an errant punch which broke Viola's collarbone; they visited the Emergency Room; and finally both agreed to start over and *really* work things out.

The pattern of a major breakdown in the relationship followed by a reconciliation occurred with increasing regularity. For Viola, the reality of a failed relationship thus became increasingly difficult to ignore. The relationship staggered on and on, finally into a separation, a bitter divorce, and then further abortive and painful attempts at reconciliation. For nearly two years after the divorce papers were at last signed, Viola was emotionally devastated. Only after a major career opportunity engaged her was she able to pull herself together and begin the life she now happily embraces. Three years after her divorce, she is certain she should have ended the relationship many years earlier.

The Case in Perspective

Viola's case is a prototype of relationships where the partners suffer through a string of painful discoveries before making the big discovery that the situation is untenable. The impact of recognizing failure is a "punch"—an apt term, for relationships like Viola's go on like old-fashioned bare-knuckle prizefights, round following round and ending only when one of the contestants is too bloody and beaten to continue. A sudden or overwhelming Realization typically helps end a relationship simply because something becomes too devastating to rationalize or otherwise ignore.

KNOCKOUT REALITY

The cases of Dade Loftgren and Florence Waits are interesting examples of successful quits. Like Viola, both remained for many years in unhealthy relationships (Dade for five years and Florence for over twenty), and both relied heavily upon myths to permit them to carry on with outward dignity. However, both Dade and Florence had sudden Realizations that caused them abruptly to decide to end their marriages and cut short their unhappiness.

SORRY, GOD

While it is easy to visualize a sudden decision to end a relationship occurring in the midst of a screaming argument or in the agony of the discovery of infidelity, what distinguishes the story of Dade Loftgren is that his Realization came while he was sitting

on his patio in quiet contemplation. It was in every way, save for
his Realization, an ordinary day. What also makes his story so
engaging is that he was keeping a daily journal of his feelings;
thus Dade's story is uncommonly precise and detailed, including the account in his own words of the myths that failed him.
His journal contains this recollection of the evening of his
Realization:

> A chill moved along my spine. It moved slowly, as if it,
> too, was weary. I sat in Tucson, Arizona, on July 11, 1978
> (hardly chill weather at ninety-plus degrees in the early
> night), but my mind was in San Diego, watching myself lie
> face down in a damp ravine.

Sitting in Arizona, Dade was remembering San Diego as it was
on the afternoon of the second day of his marriage, nearly five
years before. He wondered if anything had really changed.

Still in college when he married, Dade had placed great faith
in knowledge. Determined to have the perfect marriage, he purchased a copy of the *Guide to Successful Marriage*, which his new
wife read aloud as they drove to California the first full day of
their honeymoon. The book, although logical and well written,
was to be of no help.

Dade and the new Mrs. Loftgren, née Teresa Johnson, arrived
at Harbor Island in San Diego in midafternoon. After admiring
the view from their seventh-floor room in the Harbor Sheraton,
Dade led Teresa to the bed and abruptly pushed her onto it. She
gasped when she hit, for it gave way under her and rolled her
over. The desk captain had guessed it was their honeymoon (or
perhaps it was on the travel agent's record), for he had given the
Loftgren's the hotel's one water bed.

Both Dade and Teresa secretly believed that they should be
setting sexual records on their honeymoon, feeling the weight of
coming decades filled with salacious questions about their first
week as a married couple. The previous night they had
exhausted each other making love, rested, then exhausted each
other again.

Worried that he might become seasick on the rolling bed,
Dade decided to hurry; he turned Valentino serious, covering

Teresa with wet kisses. When he finished with what he felt were
the essentials of foreplay, including undressing them both, he
positioned himself above her.

She pulled him into her, then abruptly pushed him away,
wincing with pain. The endurance sex of the previous night had
left her sore, and she seemed to blame him, for she turned away
in anger. He tried, but failed, to soothe her.

Dade did not understand, but he had been repeatedly
cautioned that men were not capable of comprehending women,
particularly the one to whom they were married. Recalling
sound advice carefully learned, he decided that she needed privacy and time to "let the storm pass." He kissed her lightly,
dressed, kissed her again, and left.

Dade remembered it as one of the flawless afternoons mass
produced in southern California. Between the sea breeze and
the sight of the massive navy vessels headed into harbor Dade
almost forgot he was married.

Upon returning to the hotel he was surprised to find the door
to the room chained. Through the two-inch crack he strained to
see Teresa. Dade's journal tells the story:

> I pressed my face to the crack and put on a deep voice. I
> said, "It's room service, madam. I'm delivering the tongue
> you ordered." And I stuck my tongue into the crack.
> No response.
> I knocked. "Hey, wake up."
> "Just a minute." Her voice was without life.
> I drew a deep breath and expelled it, hoping to blow
> away my frustration. I had been a Boy Scout, first in my
> catechism class, and knew Jesus Christ on a first-name
> basis. I was skilled at controlling myself. Teresa arrived to
> unlatch the chain, then turned and walked back to the
> bed without meeting my eyes.
> "Perfect day," I said, as if addressing a stranger. She lay
> face down, silent.
> "What the hell is wrong with you?" I finally asked.
> "You wouldn't understand."
> "Probably not. This is your honeymoon, you know.

This is fucking beautiful California, you know."

"I knew you were mad."

"I'm getting there. Nice work."

"That's it. Blame me. Everything is my fault." She at last turned to face me. "Just because you beat me up with your thing, you're mad at me."

"Christ."

"Just get out. Get out." She spun away so quickly that tears flew off her face like sweat off a hit boxer.

"Fine. I'll just get my stuff together and move into the bathroom."

Teresa spun back around. "Look, I'll never be what you want. I can't be everything. I can't be married to you. Just get out. I'm taking a plane home tonight."

That day, five years earlier, had been the first time Teresa had threatened to leave. Of course she hadn't left, at least not for good. Indeed, that day in San Diego was only the first of what was to be a consistent pattern in their relationship. Teresa's moodiness and her love of a good fight were to become for Dade a major source of displeasure; he felt that the roller-coaster swings in happiness undermined their marriage. Dade had never figured out how to avoid such episodes, nor had he learned to accept them.

In San Diego Dade had argued with Teresa about her leaving, struggling to figure out what he had done wrong. Finally, overcome with frustration, he had bolted from the hotel room. As the door to the elevator opened, so did the door to their room. Teresa stepped into the hallway and said timidly, "Come back."

As Dade walked to her, she ran to him, threw her arms around his neck, squeezed him, and begged him to forgive her. He had assured her he would. "It's forgotten," his journal reports he said. Still, he had never forgiven her, nor forgotten even one detail of that day. Undoubtedly, if the incident had ended in the hallway of the Sheraton his pledge to forget would have been upheld; however, the unseen wheel that dictated the cycles of their relationship was only beginning its revolution. Yet to come was the moment in the damp ravine that in recollection could still send chills through Dade.

Still standing in the hotel corridor, with Teresa's tears wetting his collar, Dade felt a need to get away from the scene of their unseemly behavior and suggested that they take a drive to Balboa Park.

Balboa Park might well have been designed to make one forget anything unseemly. Whereas the great cathedrals were said to be designed to remind the visitor of his puniness before God, the trees and gardens of Balboa Park were seemingly planned to make the visitor feel part of Eden.

Dade was cheered; he busied himself with his most treasured wedding gift, the 35-mm Minolta camera from his best friend. As they ventured into one of the wilderness areas of the park, Teresa stopped and said she wanted to talk about their marriage. Dade's journal best tells the story:

> "I'm not so sure I can be a good wife," she began slowly. "At least, I'm not sure I can be the wife you expect me to be. Now we're married, and I want you to know that you cannot and will not change me . . . ever."
>
> There was fight in her words, but I refused to notice. I tried to explain that I just wanted to make her happy. I told her my belief that everyone changes continually. I told her that if a person is aware, he can help ensure that the inevitable change will be positive, will be growth. I knew I was lecturing, but Teresa was staring at me and listening, so I proceeded. I explained the microcosm theory: Each individual has the forces of evil and good wrestling within him, each life playing out the eternal struggle.
>
> Her reply was ironic: "I don't want your philosophy. What I want is to be Teresa Johnson [her maiden name] . . . er, Teresa Loftgren [her married name], I mean. Shit, I want to be me, that's all."
>
> I stayed philosophical and talked of changing and choosing. I could see she wasn't following me, and was annoyed. So I ended my little speech with a question: "Am I talking sense?" Expectantly, I waited for my new bride to reply.
>
> "You're full of shit."

I hoped she was joking, but nobody laughed. "Sometimes I am," I told her. "But the belief in what I said runs through every cell in my body."

"Then every cell in your body is full of shit. I'm sorry I married you." She spoke each word slowly and distinctly so that each one was a separate cut. She turned and walked away.

I was stunned. The will drained from my body. The camera fell from my hands. The next thing I knew my back was wet from the long damp grass. Teresa raced to my side.

She seemed disappointed to find me conscious. She glared at me and said, "Quit being dramatic."

"Just go away," I whispered. When she obeyed and walked away, I was incensed. I leaped to my feet, found the camera, and hurled it at her.

Since he had never been a violent man, Dade's camera throwing was imperfect; he missed by a wide margin. Indeed, Dade had never thrown anything in anger before, let alone anything as precious as this favorite wedding gift. Predictably, his own violence scared him. He ran. It was uncontrolled running, and within a minute he had twice stumbled and fallen. The second time he made no effort to rise.

Teresa again rushed to his side. She wept. She apologized. She spoke of her unending love for Dade. Held like a six-foot doll, Dade stared at the clouds and wondered why God had deserted his child.

This story—his story—played through Dade's mind that July night in Arizona. The cold of the wet San Diego grass became too real; Dade had to force his thoughts back to the hot Arizona night.

Though the events of that honeymoon afternoon in San Diego still struck Dade as inexplicable, what followed perplexed him even more. Teresa was apparently unaffected by the scene in the park, for she seemed genuinely happy for the remainder of the trip. Dade had been puzzled and hurt, but managed to carry on as if nothing had happened. He even continued to take pictures, although he could not be sure the camera was functioning.

Once they returned to Tucson they laughed at all the new-lywed jokes and happily recounted the sights of the trip. Neither Dade nor Teresa mentioned the afternoon in the park until, months later, Dade casually recalled the events for Teresa. She barely remembered the incident, and dismissed it airily.

For five years Dade had been perplexed by Teresa's readiness to forget. Screaming, insults, threats—nothing seemed to affect her for more than a moment. Early in their marriage Dade had learned they had very different standards as to what was even classified as an argument. Dade had told Teresa in the midst of a screaming session that if they had one more argument that month, he was moving out. Her startled reply was, "We're not arguing, you asshole."

"What do you call it?" he had asked.

"A discussion," she, of course, replied.

"We're yelling. We're angry. We're arguing," he countered.

"You don't know anything about arguing."

And she was right, for Dade had an inordinate amount yet to learn.

On the night Dade had his Realization, he had ended another argument by retreating to the heat of the patio. He had been sitting in the heat for nearly an hour and he allowed self-pity to overtake him. As he had done so often, he wondered how he had gotten himself into this marriage. Long ago he had admitted to himself that Teresa had been right—he had wanted to change her, particularly her moodiness. When they met, he had believed that people can and do change. Furthermore, he believed that by changing himself, by perfecting himself, he could change those around him. If only he could be good and strong and positive, he would evoke a reaction in kind. "Your world is a mirror of yourself," he had told anyone who complained about the way they were treated. Now he was complaining to himself. Circumstances do matter.

Teresa slid the patio door open and stood in the doorway. She asked if Dade was coming to bed. Dade remembers her extending her hand, motioning for him to come to her. He describes his reaction:

I rose and walked toward her. As I walked the length of

the patio, I felt strangely as if I was in the hallway of the Sheraton Hotel in San Diego. She put her arms around me and pressed her face into my chest. "I'm sorry," she whispered. Five years—no change. As she pressed against me, I looked to the heavens, just as I had done in the ravine. How many more years of fighting? I told God I was sorry, but I was giving up. I gave it my best for five years, but I wasn't going on. She pulled me toward the bedroom. I followed, but I wasn't the same man.

The Case in Perspective

Dade Loftgren had his Realization that night in Arizona. He spent six months trying to talk himself out of demanding a divorce but failed. The Realization was too powerful. What was so haunting about his awakening was not the discovery that the marriage had problems—that came on the honeymoon—but that the relationship was not going to change.

Dade's case can be summarized as follows:

- High expectations had been combined with great optimism and mythology.

- A quiet but stunning Realization that optimism was unwarranted forced a complete reexamination of the "It'll work out" myth.

- The oft-postponed decision to quit, when finally made, was a clear, controlled decision.

- After a fairly brief adjustment, both parties felt substantial improvement in their lives.

The most positive and useful Realizations are those like Dade Loftgren's; the experience becomes an integral part of reevaluating the relationship's future and thus a cornerstone in the process of making a decision. In successful quits the Realization often becomes not a guiding star but a kind of trailing star (a South Star perhaps?) providing reassurance that the right path was taken, reducing doubt, regret, guilt.

RECYCLED PROMISES

In its broader sense the story of Florence Waits is the story of how the two extremes exemplified by Dade and Viola—Dade's controlled and successful quit following a strong, introspective insight, and Viola's staggering, almost endless failure to realize the whole truth—are combined in one quitting situation.

Florence was married for twenty-five years—nearly as long as Viola—but unlike Viola, for most of the time Florence was happy. After seventeen or eighteen years of marriage the pressures on Florence's husband, Roger, as corporate vice-president competing to be president, became too great a burden; he began to escape through alcohol. Within a year he passed from being a social drinker to being an alcoholic. Florence noticed the change, but like Roger was slow to label it alcoholism. Yet, when Roger went from buying individual half-gallon bottles of Scotch to buying half-gallons by the case, Florence was concerned. Her loving concern only exacerbated the problem, because Roger, who loved her, tried to hide his drinking, which only meant that he was rarely home during waking hours. He would say that he was "working late" in order to have the time for drinks after work or would "take a little drive alone" in order to drink in the evening. Roger's absences brought anger, resentment, arguments, and withdrawal to the relationship.

Roger was able to carry on in his corporate role successfully. Florence ran a profitable dress shop. Both retreated into their careers. Both saw the distance between them grow, but both said it was temporary. Roger would lick his drinking problem "someday." They diverted themselves with material indulgences, like the day they bought two new cars—a Cadillac for him, a Pontiac for her.

Florence's conviction that "things would work out" was damaged one September afternoon when one of her customers noticed her name badge and asked if she knew a man named Roger Waits. Florence laughed and acknowledged she knew him well—Roger was her husband. The customer told her she managed the Continental Apartments where Roger had his apartment. Florence disguised her surprise; she knew nothing about an apartment. Not a suspicious woman, Florence tried to forget what she had learned; perhaps the woman was mistaken. That evening, when Roger finally arrived home, she would not let herself ask. But the next afternoon she was overcome by a desire to drive out to the apartment complex. She was not sure just where it was or what she expected to see, but she found herself driving through the neighborhood around the Continental Apartments, which was not far from downtown Kansas City. Florence described the events:

> My family had always told me that I was a little bit psychic. I was just following an impulse by driving out there. And then on impulse I turned down this alley. The trash bins said Continental Apartments. Just as I had convinced myself that I was a fool to be out playing Dick Tracy—you know, reading trash bins in some strange alley—I saw Roger opening the car door of his new Cadillac for another woman—one of my best customers and a friend of mine, for Christ's sake!
>
> I pulled my car in so they couldn't get out. Meanwhile, they saw me, and this woman locked the doors . . . those electric locks. I guess I couldn't blame her because I had some of my tools, my sewing and alterations things, and I just grabbed a pair of scissors when I got out of my car. I ran over and tried to get at her. Roger was sitting inside yelling at me through the glass, and she was curled up on the floor of the car screaming, and I was beating on the car with my scissors. You know, you do go crazy.

Roger managed to get his car past Florence's. Florence stayed beside the Cadillac, still stabbing it with her scissors. When Roger got clear of the alley, Florence ran back to her car. A true-life chase scene was underway.

It was five o'clock—rush-hour traffic—so Florence caught Roger when he stopped for a light at a major intersection. Still enraged, Florence put her bumper against his and pushed, determined to drive him into the rushing cross traffic. Fortunately, the Pontiac was no match for the Cadillac's weight and brakes; Florence merely filled the air with smoke from her spinning tires. It was a few miles before Florence and her Pontiac got another shot at Roger and his Cadillac, this time on a quiet side street. Roger slowed down and motioned for Florence to pull alongside. She did so, but then swerved into the side of his car, bouncing him onto the curb. She backed up, then lurched forward into his car.

Roger was again lucky to have had the heavier car, for Florence so smashed the front of her Pontiac that she couldn't drive on, allowing Roger to escape before any bones were broken. The next day Florence sued for divorce.

By the end of the week Roger had persuaded her to give him another chance, promising to stop drinking and to give up the other woman.

Thus, as in Viola's case, the discovery of infidelity led to a commitment to start anew. But again adultery was only a symptom of a failed relationship. It was not possible to start over; after more than twenty years, the behavior patterns were simply too rigid to alter dramatically by promises alone. Unlike Viola, Florence was able to admit to herself the possibility that her problems could not be solved by waiting and hoping. This admission allowed Florence to open her options, and she took the novel approach of both preparing for divorce *and* making a final dramatic effort to save the marriage. She put their money into new accounts under her name, made inquiries into the requisite legal procedures for divorce, and planned her life as a single woman. But she also threw herself into a campaign designed to obviate those preparations: She solicited help from every possible source—two doctors, Roger's friends and co-workers, and Alcoholics Anonymous.

After ten to twelve weeks, she sensed the salvage effort was failing. Worse, their arguments had started to turn violent. During one of them, Roger so frightened both Florence and himself by briefly choking her that he disappeared into the night.

Florence spent that night deep in depression; she could not bring herself to leave her sick husband but could not be happy married to him. She alternated between thoughts of running away and dreams of new plans to rescue Roger and their marriage.

Roger appeared the next morning at the dress shop. He delighted Florence with a ruby and diamond ring. He sat her down and swore to start over—to give up drinking and become once again a complete husband. Roger sensed that Florence wanted to believe him and he gave her the appeal he knew had moved her before. He said, "With your help, Flo, I know we can lick this. I know we can." Florence recalls having had an odd feeling of having been through the same experience before. But it was not a *déjà vu*. Those were the same words Roger had spoken the week following the auto chase when she had agreed not to divorce him. She hid it from Roger, but in that instant of recognition she had the Realization that led to the end of their marriage.

The Case in Perspective

It was suggested earlier that Florence's story was an interesting combination of those of Viola and Dade. Like Viola, Florence had a long marriage and had suffered through a series of painful incidents, refusing to accept failure. Florence would have experienced the same unhappy ending as Viola, save for a blow of unmistakable reality. Like Dade, she suddenly realized what had *not* happened—that "things" had not "worked out" and never would. With great sorrow, Florence again filed for divorce. This second time she would not be dissuaded.

While Florence did not bounce into a glamorous or fun-filled new life—she was middle-aged and alone and did not want to be—she never doubted for a minute the wisdom of her decision. She was able to put together a pleasant, if quiet, life without Roger. Meanwhile, she was able to observe the unfolding of the future she had decided against. Roger married a woman considered to be much like Florence; mutual friends kept Florence informed of the life she could have had. Even with a new wife and a new home Roger could not start over; he never did lick his alcoholism. He left his job, blew all his money, and was dead at forty-six from alcohol-related medical problems. A clean punch from reality saved Florence from years of misery and the loss of her material wealth.

REALITY AND THE CAREER QUIT

Changing jobs can be a simple or a painful decision, but leaving a career is nearly always a wrenching emotional experience, rarely undertaken without fear, pain, and anger. A new job can mean as little as plying the identical skills in a similar office in an adjoining building, the only noticeable change a slightly larger paycheck with a different company name at the top. Or it can mean a different city (or country), a different industry, major new responsibilities (or, in a more painful change, greatly lessened responsibilities), and a company with a radically different personality.

Most job changes are within the same career and hence involve location more than production—regardless of the changes in environment, the work is similar. More important, job changes within a career do not typically involve grave changes in self-image. In contrast, leaving a career means walking away from the skills that defined a person for the world. Friendships founded on the kinship of profession are given up. Substantial changes in monetary position often result. Overall, every relationship is thrown into question until the changing individual establishes a new identity and new relationships.

The pain associated with choosing to leave a career is closely related to the commercial isolation of the work skills. Two examples of extremely isolated professional skills, both demanding years of specialized training, are teaching and the ministry. In later chapters, the case of an ex-priest and that of a former Baptist minister will be examined in detail. For the purpose of studying a Realization, the story of Donna Byron, a former schoolteacher, is useful.

WAKE UP AND QUIT

Donna is a small, sweet woman with sad brown eyes. She is not a person to assert herself, but quitting, to be successful, must be an assertive act. For years Donna fought admitting that she was aware she had chosen the wrong career. When she finally acknowledged the reality of her mistake, she moved with assurance into a happier life. Her Realization was important to her decision and success.

Exploring the events that lead to major decisions in life, such as a marriage or the choice of career, make it clear why there is a need for so many quitting decisions. Rarely are the critical "decisions" in life really conscious choices; even more rarely are they well-informed or careful decisions. Donna explains how she "chose" teaching:

> I never grew up wanting to be a teacher; it just kinda happened. I started out taking psychology classes, but ended up taking education classes. In my day you became either a nurse, a teacher, or a wife. The things I was interested in studying, like psychology, just weren't practical. I didn't have any prospects for a husband, and I didn't want to work nights in some hospital, so I got a degree in teaching. I told myself I'd only be teaching a year or two, then get married and have a family. I was wrong about the getting married and the family. I went on year after year waiting for my life to change, but it stayed the same.
>
> After three years of teaching, I went to Europe to teach in a private school. That lasted four years, and I loved it, but when I got back to the States, I thought I'd try something else, something besides teaching. No way. I'd been teaching for nine years by then. What else could I do? I was a clerk in a clothing store. I was a slave in a day-care center. Within six months I was back in a school, teaching.

Donna was back in teaching, but her sentiments were divided between gratitude and resentment. She was told she was lucky to have an ideal teaching position when teaching jobs were at a premium. With considerable effort, she decided she was happy.

As is common when doubts are forcibly repressed rather than examined and resolved, Donna was vulnerable to startling glimpses of her predicament. She describes her first revelation.

> I decided, at long last, that I was going to be teaching for a while, and I should treat it as a profession. The county required a master's degree to move to the next pay scale.

So I threw myself into the master's program. It took three years, but I not only got the damn degree, I also got perfect grades along the way. It exhausted me, but I did it.

I got that degree at the end of my tenth year of teaching. When I came back for the eleventh year, with my wonderful master's degree already framed and hanging in my bedroom, I opened my first paycheck and saw all of seventeen dollars a week more. I guess I should have known what to expect, but when it was there, it seemed to shout out to me that teaching was a dead end.

I would work and work, and the girls who did absolutely nothing made the same salary. Here I had resigned myself to supporting myself, but hard work meant nothing. I said to myself, "That does it."

Following her first strong Realization, Donna began the disheartening task of choosing a new career. Because she had decided to finish the school year, she had nine months to prepare for the change—also nine months of temptation to forget leaving and decide to continue teaching. By spring Donna had discovered that while her master's-degree raise was minuscule, her salary as a senior teacher was well above entry-level jobs in other fields. Returning to graduate school was also out, financially and emotionally. The Realization that had come with her paycheck began to seem distant. Change was expensive and frightening. Teaching was penultimate security.

Donna later wondered if there wasn't something providential about her next Realization, for it came just as she was ready to resign herself to teaching.

My birthday came along and they threw a joint party for me and another teacher who happened to have the same birthday, but who was ten years older. I hadn't realized the other teacher had the same birthday. During the party I just sat there and stared at her, knowing I was looking at myself in the future. I got this feeling that I wasn't going to be around when I was ten years older.

Then I got the feeling I wasn't going to be around for my *next* birthday.

That party set me off. For two weeks I sat up all night crying. I was lost. I talked to friends, and they said I'd be a fool to leave. My mother told me not to be a "ninny."

After two weeks of worrying, I cried myself to sleep one night, and the next morning I woke up and knew for sure I was going to quit. I'm not sure how I knew, but I knew.

It took Donna another two weeks to work up the nerve to tell her principal she was leaving. She twice walked to the office only to turn and leave without going in. Finally she did go in and said, "I'm never doing another 'Welcome to School' bulletin board." Although during her first year outside of teaching her income fell almost in half, she says her only regret is not leaving five years sooner.

The Case in Perspective

As in the successful quits in the marriage cases, Donna had strong Realization experiences that forced her to put her past and future into perspective. The Realizations have since served Donna as mental amulets, keeping guilt and doubt away.

REALIZATION AND QUITTING IN POLITICS

Political popularity tends to be evanescent; hence, one of the great challenges in the career of a politician is to quit gracefully rather than to be thrown out of office. As in any important quitting decision, the Realization is a crucial step in the decision to depart. Political figures are subjected to an excess of advice, much of it highly critical; to grow insensitive to a reality such as fallen popularity is only natural. (Certainly the demise of Richard Nixon's career demonstrates how long a politician can deny reality.)

Two political quitting stories published in recent years have been chosen to illustrate the function of the Realization in quitting a career.

L.B.J.

During the last five years of his life Lyndon Johnson talked intimately to Doris Kearns, the author of his biography, *Lyndon Johnson and the American Dream*, about his life and his career. He told Kearns of his decision to resign the presidency rather than fight for reelection:

I felt that I was being chased on all sides by a giant stampede coming at me from all directions. On one side, the American people were stampeding me to do something about Vietnam. On another side, the inflationary economy was booming out of control. Up ahead were dozens of danger signs pointing to another summer of riots in the cities. I was being forced over the edge by rioting blacks, demonstrating students, marching welfare mothers, squawking professors, and hysterical reporters. And then the final straw. The thing I feared from the first day of my Presidency was actually coming true. Robert Kennedy had openly announced his intention to reclaim the throne in memory of his brother. And the American people, swayed by the magic of the name, were dancing in the streets. The whole situation was unbearable for me. After thirty-seven years of public service, I deserved something more than being left alone in the middle of the plain, chased by stampedes on every side.

But Johnson was not a man to run, even from a giant stampede coming from all directions. He was a man. A man should fight. Yet the fight began to seem hopeless. Kearns explains:

So Johnson found himself in an untenable position in early 1968. It was impossible to quit and impossible to stay. If he left office and went back to Texas, he would be acting like a coward; if he stayed for another four years, he would be paralyzed before his term was out. For months his position was all the more untenable. He was in the grip of that supreme despair which, as Kierkegaard says, is not to know one is in despair. No matter how hard he tried to think it out, he got nowhere.

One line of action was as bad as the other. No matter how hectic his activity, he could not drive the demons away. But then, Johnson explained, one day—exactly what day is not clear—he realized the total impossibility of his situation. The realization came to him in a dream. In the dream he saw himself swimming in a river. He was swimming from the center toward one shore. He swam and swam, but he never seemed to get any closer. He turned around to swim to the other shore, but again he got nowhere. He was simply going 'round and 'round in circles.

L.B.J. in Perspective

His dream allowed Johnson to accept the impossibility of his situation and to break the mind set that gave him only two options: (1) stay and be defeated; or (2) run and be a coward. The Realization forced him to explore alternatives, including the option he chose: to combine his resignation with a series of political initiatives intended to elevate him above the political turmoil while proving him a statesman.

DANIEL PATRICK MOYNIHAN

Political appointees have an even more immediate need to recognize their reality than do the politicians they serve, for their political appointment can end long before the next election. Daniel Patrick Moynihan spent many of his days as U.S. ambassador to the United Nations trying to decide if it was time for him to resign. Moynihan arrived at the UN feeling the "world forum" had become a shooting gallery, with the United States as the largest, most phlegmatic target. Moynihan decided to counterattack, a concept that startled, then offended, a diplomatic bureaucracy comprised largely of experts at appeasement and apologetics.

Soon discouraged by the UN, but more so by criticism and rumors of criticism from his superiors at the White House, Moynihan discussed resignation. He was dissuaded. His doubts resurfaced several months later when his leave of absence from

Harvard was about to end. He had to choose: quit Harvard or quit the United Nations. In his book about his days at the UN., *A Dangerous Place*, Moynihan speaks of his decision.

> On January 9, in Washington, after finishing our talk on the Middle East debate, I told Kissinger I would leave Harvard. It had been a wrench for him to do so, and in truth his chair had been kept open far past the normal deadline. Next to great wealth, a chair in the Harvard Department of Government was possibly the most important security a man could have in Washington. There were few posts there with greater prestige, and a professorship had the advantage of being for life. It was a guarantor, also, that one's next book would be prominently enough published, and that a generation or so of young persons would in this manner come to know who had done well and who had done badly during those Washington years.

Despite his hesitation to give up his position at Harvard, Moynihan was staying at the UN. He told President Ford so.

> I said to the President that my leave at Harvard expired this week, and that while it meant more to me than anything save my family, I would give up my professorship and stay on in the Administration through the primaries and the convention, as I did not want to do anything to hurt him. I said it may or may not be true as the *Wall Street Journal* put it that I was the most popular member of his administration, but I certainly didn't want to give any ammunition to Reagan who was constantly invoking my name.

The meeting with Ford took place on a Tuesday (January 27, 1976). By that Friday, Moynihan was writing a resignation letter. In the space of those days he had had a Realization that revealed his true relationship with Kissinger and Ford.

Even as Moynihan was meeting with Ford to offer to sacrifice his self-interest, *The New York Times* was preparing to publish the text of a document Ambassador Moynihan had issued to various

U.S. embassies around the world. As happened so often, reaction to Moynihan's ideas was intense and largely hostile. A follow-up column in the *Times* contained a single paragraph that caused Moynihan to feel he must go. This is the paragraph that changed Moynihan from self-sacrifice to resignation:

> Now Messrs. Ford and Kissinger support Moynihan in public and deplore him in private. Having put him in the job, they can neither tame nor repudiate him. He has always been the enemy of his best ideas, always used the most provocative phrases, but Mr. Kissinger knew all that before and is now having to deal with the consequences and his own regrets.

That paragraph permitted Moynihan to realize that the future held only further circumscriptions of his responsibility and freedom to express himself. It was not that criticisms from Kissinger and Ford were new to Moynihan, but he had felt an implicit agreement of full support when he had agreed to stay. One paragraph, and he knew at once he was wrong.

Daniel Patrick Moynihan in Perspective

Moynihan's Realization meant that he ceased hoping, could envision his future as ambassador to the UN, could assert his self-interest, and in general could make an informed decision whether to leave or stay.

Moynihan's Realization has the same elements as those in most successful quitting decisions: He explored all reasonable options to save the relationship, short of agreeing to conditions that would ensure his own unhappiness; he understood his future; he admitted the failure of the relationship; he was then able to move resolutely to a decision.

THE RELATION OF SUCCESSFUL QUITTING TO THE REALIZATION

Every decision to quit is preceded by some sort of Realization; the possible failure of the relationship must be confronted in order for a quit-or-not-to-quit decision to be made.

Each of the cases presented in this chapter is intended to

illustrate one of the ways in which a Realization is related to the overall success of a quitting decision.

- One important reason Viola's story ended unhappily was her failure to realize the hopelessness of her relationship. A number of experiences could have been final Realizations, but she refused to treat these examples of her failed relationship as anything but painful incidents. She chose to deal with each problem rather than with the *source* of the problems.

- The case of Dade Loftgren was an example of someone who was fully cognizant all along of the overall shortcomings of the relationship—he had begun to discover them during his honeymoon. *What was suddenly realized was his inability to change his marriage.*

- Florence, when she recognized her husband's old promises being recycled, knew that her efforts to mend their relationship could not succeed. As with Dade, a clear Realization of the failures of the relationship and of the impossibility of correcting them preceded the decision to quit.

- The stories of Donna Byron (the teacher), Daniel Patrick Moynihan, and President Johnson revealed the same pattern as the marriage relationships. The critical discovery was not that the relationship had problems, but that no solution could be found. The Realization was an admission of hopelessness, a rejection of the modern myths that one could—and should—rise above circumstances.

THE REALIZATION IN THE CONTEXT OF THE QUITTING DECISION

As explained in the introduction, all individuals interviewed during the research for this book were given a score for the "success" of their quits (based on how quickly they were able to adjust to the end of the relationship, how much regret they felt, and how likely they would be to make the same decision again).

Each quit was also broken down into its components, and each component was also given a score. The strength of the Realization was one of the components scored.

THE RULE

The score for the strength, or "punch," of the Realization was based on the individual's recognition of the experience as a major turning point, the remembered impact of the insight, and the suddenness of the insight (see page 13). In sum, the score for "Realization" is a subjective measure of the experience in terms of how close it came to a sudden, overwhelming understanding that the relationship had failed and could not be saved.

As the preceding cases showed, there is a strong correlation between the "success" score of the quit and the "punch" score of the Realization. The stronger the Realization, the greater the likelihood of a successful quit.

EXCEPTIONS TO THE RULE

In addition to identifying factors that tend to result in constructive quitting, a careful analysis was undertaken of the specific instances where the general pattern does *not* hold. Several individuals reported that they had had a *strong* Realization but had made the *wrong decision* by quitting.

Examination of these aberrant scores (what statisticians call outliers) revealed a consistent difference in the nature of the Realization. In each case, what was scored as a strong Realization was really an angry, impulsive outburst that had resulted in an abrupt quit. Rather than a sudden discovery that the relationship *could not be saved*—a discovery almost inevitably filled with great sorrow—the exceptional cases were unpleasant incidents, filled with anger.

What makes an angry incident akin to a Realization is the likelihood that the angry individual will turn on the overall relationship, reciting each flaw in it. However, in successful quits the Realization is a *secondary* discovery (that efforts *to change* the relationship have failed) rather than a primary discovery of flaws (which signals a need for a change).

Here are two brief examples of impulsive, angry quits that contrast dramatically with the successful quits presented earlier.

Margaret

Margaret is a loquacious, demanding woman but an attractive and witty one as well. Two years ago one of her friends was struggling through a marriage that was turning cruel. Margaret generously invited her friend to stay with her and her husband, Ralph, until some solution could be found. Three weeks into the friend's stay Margaret was called upon to stay with a sick relative. In her absence Ralph and the house guest made love, which Margaret learned the following morning, when the guilt-ridden friend confessed. Margaret moved into an apartment that same day and looked into getting a divorce the next. She ignored her husband's apologies and "explanations."

Margaret had immediately felt that her marriage was untenable. Only months later, after the divorce, was she able to recognize that while her husband had made a major mistake, the marriage had in all other ways been strong and healthy. Margaret began to deeply regret her decision to quit. She began seeing her ex-husband, and they are now planning to remarry.

Victoria

Greatness was demanded of Victoria, a child of wealth and talent. She was named for her aunt, a poet of minor celebrity. Victoria's greatest childhood achievements came when she was seated with a cello. For fourteen years she practiced four to six hours daily and was accepted as a pupil by a succession of accomplished cellists. However, virtuosity eluded her.

In her early twenties Victoria began to study with a particularly demanding, petulant teacher. If she played a passage poorly, he would order her from the room, abruptly ending the day's lesson. Having one day been insulted at length and commanded to depart, Victoria practiced until dawn, repeating a passage until her hands finally agreed to execute it properly. She was tense for the next lesson and became more so the closer her playing brought her to those troublesome bars. She did not make it; she made the same error she had made the day before. Her instructor raged, telling her he was failing her for the week, perhaps for the whole semester. Again he insisted she leave.

Shaken, crestfallen, then angry, Victoria left not only the lesson but also the cello. For eleven years Victoria did not touch a cello, feeling uncomfortable at even the sight of one. She quickly discovered she had lost an important and valuable part of her life, but having declared herself, she stubbornly refused to reconsider her decision to quit.

After an eleven-year hiatus Victoria again plays the cello, although she will not let anyone listen. In retrospect she realizes that she had options short of quitting: changing instructors, playing only for enjoyment, or otherwise changing her goals. She understands now that her decision was irrational and cost her dearly. She openly laments the years of enjoyment she lost and the possible career she gave away.

Two characteristics distinguish the Realizations of those who were *correct* in their decision to quit from those who were *incorrect*: (1) the Realizations leading to successful quits tend to be the discovery not of problems but of the inability to resolve problems; and (2) the Realizations in successful quits tend to be a sad giving up, rather than an angry denunciation.

The Realization in Perspective

One reason the experience of the Realization is closely related to the success of a quit is that it is tied in with the other important components of the quitting process. When we examine the correspondences between the Realization and other key factors in a quit, we see that the strength of the Realization is directly connected to the three other components that affect success: Futuring—the ability to envision the relationship's future; the analysis of Self-interest; and the Clean Decision to quit. Together, these form a *Gestalt* of positive change.

FUTURING—THE

PREDICTABILITY OF

RELATIONSHIPS

ONE fascinating, if frustrating, aspect of research on social or psychological issues is the simultaneous simplicity and profundity of the findings. Once the answer to a question about a social issue is available, if it is stated clearly and logically, it seems so commonsensical that on hearing the results one wonders why any research was needed. An example is the question "What class—upper-, middle-, or lower-income—has the highest rate of mental disorder?" Given any of the three answers and an explanation, the likely response is, "Well, that seems obvious." If you are told that the answer is the upper class, because they have not only the pressures of "life at the top" but the best medical care and thus the greatest likelihood of a disorder being uncovered, labeled, and reported, the reply is, "That seems obvious." Yet if you are told, instead, that the answer is the lower class, because mental disorders are related to poor nutrition in infancy, the reply is the same, "That seems obvious." (Perhaps the "that seems obvious" phenomenon explains why so many researchers resort to arcane mathematics or jargon. One economist, for instance, insists that all of his discipline is "common sense made difficult.")

So it is with one simple secret to deciding whether to quit or stay: the easy, obvious (and incomplete) answer to the problem of whether or not to quit is to confront the future honestly,

mentally composing the most realistic short story possible that
will predict the course of the existing relationship. The author of
that story must then decide if he or she wants to live the life of
the story's main character. If not, and if the person cannot envision a reasonable course of action that would make the future
desirable, then that becomes the Realization; the person asserts
his or her Self-interest and executes a Clean Decision to quit.

See the future. Take it or leave it. This simple, profound
process, referred to here as Futuring, would seem to be the
obvious "secret" of successful quitting.

Naturally, this is too easy. But the real weakness of the easy
answer is *not* the obvious one—an inability to foresee the future.
Indeed, while the years ahead seem shrouded in mystery, individuals were frequently encountered during the course of this
research who, in a letter or diary, had written their expectations
for a relationship's future and who, without exception, had as-
tounded themselves with their prescience. Upon reflection, this
is not surprising. Most individuals can accurately assess the *current* state of a relationship and have some idea of its positive or
negative *trend*. With these two pieces of information, the basic
story line of the future is known. Possible major occurrences that
might alter the relationship can then be incorporated, as their
likelihood warrants. Because the person composing this story
will be one of the major characters in the real-life dénouement,
that character's actions will be predicted more readily and to
some extent his or her future will act out the prophecy because it
was made—prediction becomes destiny. Thus a reliable guess
can be made about what the future is likely to be.

The fundamental weakness of the easy answer is, of course, its
ease: Simple techniques are not conducive to making and implementing tough, painful decisions. To execute a successful
quit, seeing must lead to believing; believing must lead to acting.
These are treacherous steps, requiring conviction and courage,
not simplemindedness.

In his novel *The Professor of Desire*, Philip Roth's main character
marries, "at a moment of impasse and exhaustion," a woman
with whom he has lived for three less-than-blissful years. Roth's
character explains the paradox of *knowing from the start his future
of inevitable failure*: "We marry, and, as I should have known and

couldn't have known and probably always knew, mutual criticism and disapproval continue to poison our lives."
In relationships, as in physics, the Law of Inertia duly, monotonously, ineluctably applies. A relationship changes only when one of the parties to it changes. Roth's character daydreams of the possibility of a bold move that would remake his marriage: "The months go by and we remain together, wondering if a child would somehow resolve this crazy deadlock . . . or an antique shop of her own for Helen [his wife] . . . or a jewelry shop . . . or psychotherapy for us both." But nothing changes until a series of incidents leads to a Realization: "Yet I can never leave her, nor she me, not, that is, until outright disaster makes it simply ludicrous to go on waiting for the miraculous conversion of the other." Roth's character represents the common dilemma of being caught in an untenable relationship, hoping and waiting, but ignoring the future. If hopelessness is to rescue a person from an unsatisfactory relationship, the future must be not merely glimpsed but contemplated, made sufficiently real to become a Realization.

Time travel is a popular science fiction device, often incorporating a "time machine." In these stories there always seems to be a single rule for travelers headed into history: that they could only observe and would be able to do nothing to alter the course of events. Individuals often treat their futures with the same reverent impotence. They are not merely captured in a self-fulfilling prophecy, there is not even that indirect control. Rather, they are content to be unfilled self-prophets, knowing and waiting . . . forever waiting.

Being able to envision a future is singularly important in the typical successful quit, but it doesn't ensure that one will then make a satisfactory decision either to embrace or to alter that future. Here are the ways an individual can negate the value of a clear-eyed look at what lies ahead:

- An individual seeing the unhappy future for a relationship may discount the possibility, hoping for miracles. With this attitude it is unlikely that he or she will reach the Realization that not only is the relationship untenable but it will not improve.

- An individual who foresees a disastrous future and realizes the hopelessness of the relationship can still feel emotionally or circumstantially unable to implement a quit. This possibility will be discussed in the chapter devoted to the cleanness of the quitting decision.

- Some who know they confront a sad future and are capable of leaving choose not to, feeling a responsibility to someone else in the relationship. A chapter on self-interest in quitting includes a complete analysis of this kind of situation.

(A dour existentialist suggested a fourth reason for choosing to stay in a relationship fated to be unhappy: The other alternatives could all be even worse. Choosing the narrow and tautological response, the "least unhappy" alternative must then be the very same alternative as the "most happy": The criteria on which a decision is based would be the same. A more profound reply is that if all futures, whether quitting or staying, lead ineluctably to unhappiness, a more basic quitting decision is needed; for example, if leaving a marriage is as dark a prospect as staying unhappily married, an even broader quitting decision—say, quitting a whole life-style—is called for.)

While Futuring alone may not ensure success, it is perhaps the single most important aspect of the quitting decision, for it is a force stronger than hope. The case studies in this chapter will relate experiences that should make vivid the role of Futuring in the lives of individuals faced with an important quitting situation.

LIFE WITHOUT A FUTURE: "DUBIN'S LIVES"

What happens to a relationship in the absence of a recognition of the future? Describing a quitting decision as faced by a person who refuses to consider his future is a bit like trying to describe what a blind man sees; without some sense of choosing alternative futures there usually is no decision, no meaningful and purposeful action, no guided and self-possessed quit.

The purest tragedy is a story of a terrible deed made worse for its having been predicated on a mistake: Oedipus kills an old man he later learns was his father; Othello murders Desdemona on the incorrect assumption she has cuckolded him. Great tragedy can also be the story of great misdeeds: Macbeth needs only the promise of the weird sisters to plot the death of Duncan (a deed Macbeth himself calls so horrible "that tears shall drown the wind"). The irony of the modern American tragedy is that it involves neither great deeds nor misdeeds; it is the tragedy of self-delusion rather than mistaken identity, inaction rather than assault.

From the master of the portrait of desperation, Bernard Malamud, the marriage of two of his characters has been chosen to illustrate life in a prison with unlocked doors, the story of two people in a hurtful but readily escapable relationship who refuse to see the future. Malamud's most recent and most depressing novel, *Dubin's Lives*, is a particularly poignant example of an American tragedy. Malamud's William Dubin lives in the rural northeastern United States, far from war or court intrigue. Dubin isn't killed, nor does he kill anyone; instead, the wounds and suffering are of the psychological variety. The tragedy of *Dubin's Lives* is inaction: Dubin refuses to decide between his wife and his mistress; Kitty, Dubin's wife, is openly miserable, but doesn't leave Dubin; Dubin becomes impotent; Kitty can't sleep; Dubin, a biographer, can't write. In sum, no one decides, no one acts. In lieu of acting to change their lives, the characters analyze each other's failings, caught in the downward spiral of greater hurts and further retreats. Malamud gives us a lengthy look at the life Dubin and his wife share:

> Her familiar insecurities made him impatient, preachy; Dubin's incensed her. They argued about taste, habit, idiosyncrasy. Both guarded their defenses. There were differences concerning timing, efficiency, sex. Don't explain sex to me, Kitty cried. Then explain it to me, Dubin shouted. Don't be hysterical, she said. He felt confined by her limitations; she was diminished by his smallness.

This arguing represents the greatest marital intimacy we are to see, for the relationship eventually regresses into apathy and avoidance. When Dubin's mistress asks him why he stays with his wife, he replies: "There are commitments in marriage. It takes a while to reconsider." The mistress says, "You keep what you have and use anything else you can get." She is right: Dubin doesn't possess enough control over his life to make decisions—when the capacity for decision is absent, reconsideration becomes meaningless. In the novel's final line of dialogue, Fanny, Dubin's mistress, leans out a farmhouse window and calls to Dubin, "Don't kid yourself." This pathetically plain advice is something Dubin has never heeded. Dubin never admits the reality of his marriage, never has his Realization. The likely reason is Dubin's failure to consider his future. His whole life (even his career as a biographer) consists of looking back or around. Although he "writes lives," he never sees his own existence nor envisions its potential.

At only one point in the story is there an instant of insight into the future and thus, at one point, is there potential for constructive change. That moment comes when Dubin's wife (who appears to have a far worse life than Dubin, largely because she is married to him) thinks about trying something new—finding a job. She sees one future if she enters into that experiment, then she fails to seize the opportunity to act.

> "Do you think I could find work as a secretary?" she asked him. ". . . but who would want to employ a woman over fifty as a secretary?"
> "Some people would."
> "Not many."
> He thought she could make it.
> "That won't absolve you from supporting me."
> He was not expecting absolution.
> "It'll be an empty life," Kitty said.
> He said nothing.

These lines are the final scene with Dubin and his wife together. The painful irony of the line "It'll be an empty life" is that it is spoken by a woman who lives an empty life. She fails to experiment, to act, because she fears the very life she already has. Thus she is doomed. She is so wedded to her inertia that she can't imagine a better life; failing to imagine one, how can she find one? Dubin's reaction, to do and see nothing, is the completion of the irony, the fulfillment of the tragedy.

"Dubin's Lives" in Perspective

Malamud's Dubin suffers from a myopic life. Malamud never tells us why his characters are incapable of contemplating a different life, they just do not. And they cannot pursue what they cannot see. Perhaps the myopia is rooted in a sense of irreversible commitment, some attempt to freeze time at the moment of the wedding vows. Trying never to change, they grow insufferable. Perhaps there is an underlying hope that patience can replace effort. Perhaps they simply don't have the energy to pursue happiness, perhaps not the courage, perhaps not the imagination.

ZEN AND THE ART OF INACTION

There is another dangerous source of myopia, the philosophy that denies future and rejects the concept of choice. That philosophy is the Zen pursuit of life in "the present moment." Paul Williams devoted an entire page of his *Das Energi* to this observation:

> The past and future are inevitable.
> The past and the future do not exist.

John Cage says it.

> It is only irritating to think we would
> like to be somewhere else. Here we are now.

There is a Zen story that describes two boats, one with passengers and one empty, both on a rapid river. The passengers work hard to navigate their boat and eventually struggle into a safe harbor. The empty boat drifts along unguided but catches up to the occupied boat in the harbor. The moral is, of course, that we have no real control, only the illusion of control; by remaining empty and open we arrive at the same destiny as if we had planned, plotted, struggled.

This wisdom is the cliché Chinese meal: We are not long satisfied. To cease to struggle in the face of adversity and unhappiness is a questionable victory; it is the victory of the broken stallion or the trained bear. Rejecting the label of unhappiness by calling it unreal is not the same as finding happiness. Calling the future "nonexistent" and thereby rejecting the healthy benefits that come from imagining and creating a better life is to

deny a great force for positive change. As for the two boats that
arrive at the same harbor, if this refers only to death, the story is
too obvious to be profound. If it is to apply to the living, the
implication is the denial of a better future to those millions trapped in unfortunate relationships. To assert that if those trapped
millions would only accept their situation and stop struggling,
the need for change would be obviated, is wishful thinking, with
a practical value roughly equivalent to the argument that if
everyone accepted Christ, there would be no need for police.

The case that follows is an example of the kind of victory that
can be won through change.

OFF-BALANCE

It would be easy to feel sorry for Sylvia; life had given her
little with which to be happy. She is from a family that never
broke the "vicious circle of poverty." Short, big-boned, and generally unprepossessing, she was grateful when she found a
chance to marry young and relieve her family of her support.
Unfortunately, her marriage only continued the dismal life to
which she had become accustomed. She summarized the early
years:

> I had three children by the time I was twenty-one, a
> fourth at twenty-three. Two are deaf. I had no job skills,
> because I married at eighteen, right toward the end of
> high school. From the start it was a matter of survival. I
> didn't worry much about right or wrong or what I be-
> lieved in. I only believed in getting through the day.
>
> The man I married turned out to be rather unstable—
> he would just walk out on me and his family. When he
> would leave, it would be a matter of the children and I
> going on Welfare, really struggling, because when he left,
> he'd take the money. He never felt an obligation to sup-
> port his family. He would just leave, wearing whatever he
> was wearing and not come back for weeks. Once it was six
> months.
>
> When he came back, I was glad—not to see him, but
> that he would make enough money so that we could have
> meat for dinner.

When you live on Welfare, I mean without cheating, live on straight Welfare because you're too frightened to do anything you're not supposed to, and you have four children, and the most they allow you is $20 extra per week, which I earned working day-care, you're living on less than like $350 per month.

Sylvia explained why she stayed twenty years in a marriage that wedded her to misery:

Somehow I felt like if I just kept pouring everything into my marriage, it would work out. I felt like it *had* to work out. You see, I felt like I had no other options.

Like Malamud's Mr. and Mrs. Dubin, Sylvia was too intent on her pain to escape it. Unlike the educated and financially comfortable Dubins, Sylvia had nothing—except, of course, some vague hopes and the meager comfort of myths promising that perseverance would bring some reward other than early death. But Sylvia was to get something the Dubins never got: Sylvia stumbled into freedom. The magic of Sylvia's story is in the discovery by a woman—a rice-and-beans-three-times-a-day, four-children (two of them deaf), no-skills, no-connections, bum-of-a-husband woman—that she had a future. No, she didn't go on to become Margaret Mead or Betty Ford—her story is not a contribution to the literature of modern-day fairy tales—but Sylvia did put together a secure, pleasant life and perhaps even broke the poverty circle by asserting for herself and her children the existence of meaningful options. How?

To accept total responsibility for one's own life is an awesome burden, particularly when the life is so oppressive; Sylvia was typically reluctant. However, she finally sank so low that she had to look up—or, in this case, forward. With her husband gone for over three months, her telephone disconnected for nonpayment, and her house and car in danger of repossession, she finally had to acknowledge the future looming before her and was forced to change. She decided to let the house and car go if need be, to let the children assume more responsibility for each other, and to let her husband's chauvinistic attitudes be

damned—she was going to start a career. Sylvia described her
feelings:

> It was a very scary thing, the decision to go to work. I had
> to defy my husband, who I knew might return any day.
> And I had to leave the kids, even though I knew they still
> needed Mom at home. It was all very scary to me . . . you
> know . . . what could I do? And I thought of all the bills
> that my husband had run up, especially the back pay-
> ments on the house.

Sylvia was so intimidated by the future that she decided to try
to calm herself by setting it down on paper to see just what she
faced. She knew her husband's company used something called
a five-year plan to help business, so she decided that the way to
beat the monster she had never dared to face, her future, was to
attack it with a five-year plan. It worked. Her plan gave her the
confidence to act. She knew that she would lose the house and
the car, so she had to find an apartment on the bus route. She
knew that her husband would eventually return and insist that
she quit work; she planned how she would convince him it was
temporary, to let her keep the job a few more months. She also
planned to rid herself of her husband, although she would wait
until he had a decent job, so that she could have some hope of
child support. On she went, planning rather than worrying,
scheming rather than complaining. She got a job, and after a few
weeks of work the five-year plan was obsolete; she wanted more,
sooner, and started to calculate ways to accelerate her transition
to emotional and financial self-support.

> I still think to myself, "It's great to be in control." I've
> gained control over my life and my time and how I spend
> my money and my choice of clothes, and now what I fix
> for supper is what I want to eat. You know, I get to decide
> what to want and what to like.

The biggest hurdle for Sylvia and her control was still her
long-lost husband. Remembering the security she found in her
five-year plan, she again turned to pencil and paper to recapture
her convictions. Below is a "with and without" balance sheet that

she made. She has kept it for the past six years to serve as a
reminder of the strength of her feelings and to brace her resolution to resist her husband's efforts to reunite. Is is clearly subjective, angry, and self-serving, but it served her well, for somehow
to "have it in writing" intensified the truth and certified the
legitimacy of her complaint. She was prepared for battle. When
her husband returned, and returned, and returned, she didn't
weaken. Here is Sylvia's balance sheet for her marriage.

Without Husband	With Husband
Control of time	Little control of time—I'm a day person; he's a night person
Energy around myself	Life centered around him, constant drain on me
Aloneness	Loneliness
Relaxed with kids	Tension with kids—less communication, more hiding of feelings
Just enough money to get by	Uncertain income, but sometimes extra money
Good mother	Trying to live up to someone else's idea of a perfect, fantasy mother
One parent	One parent and one occasional pseudo-parent
In control of the power	Power in the hands of someone else
Trip home [the freedom to visit her parents]	
	Stroke then stab [her husband's inconsistent treatment]

"Behind every great woman there is a man who tried to stop
her."

At the bottom of Sylvia's page she had written this resolute conclusion: "Give up being his good woman. Break the addiction. Fight for my life!"

The Case in Perspective

Sylvia's story represents a victory equivalent to Sisyphus leaving his stone. For years Sylvia experimented with how best to bear the pain of a bad marriage. Then one day, that terrible-wonderful day when everything she owned was about to be lost, she wrote down her future in a five-year plan and she began to experiment in avoiding pain. She took control of her life. Poverty let one of its victims escape.

For Sylvia, the recognition of her future was her Realization. As is reflected so clearly in the balance sheet, Sylvia recognized that she must assert her Self-interest in order to be free. She made a clean quitting decision under difficult circumstances and is now leading (literally, *leading*) a much improved life.

HEART AND SOUL, BUT BODY?

It's a decision not too many people face—which sex to be—but for a few it is *the* life decision. Stella decided to quit being a man; it was the most important decision of her life, but not, she says, the most difficult.

> I was always fairly feminine. When I was in high school, I really got teased about it. The boys were always grabbing and pinching me—which I enjoyed, by the way. I always felt most at ease around the girls and knew I was attracted to the boys the same way they were. Even when I was little, I loved to stay inside and play dolls with the little girls rather than play football.
>
> But there I was in a man's body, and in high school I tried to carry on a heterosexual life. I wasn't very good at being macho, but I did occasionally try. One time I even went shopping for motorcycles—you know, a new image—but when I test-rode one, I realized they just scared me to death. I was really very feminine

Stella (at the time, George) failed to persuade himself to feel
and act like a man. He concluded that he was homosexual.

> In my late teens—I think I was eighteen—I had my first
> homosexual lover. It was heaven. From the first time I
> knew I only wanted to be with men, sexually. I wanted
> big, masculine men to take me and fill me up. Nothing is
> more gorgeous than a hard cock staring back at me.

Having homosexual lovers was exciting for Stella (George),
but he could not embrace the "homosexual life."

> In the gay community I could express my femininity—I
> let my hair grow and let my voice go as high as it wanted
> and I bought unisex clothes. I was able to be me without
> feeling the "No, No, No" eyes on my body. But I discov-
> ered I wasn't a homosexual the very first time I went to a
> gay bar.
> My first lover took me to his favorite bar. We sat there
> watching men look at each other's crotches. For three
> hours we sat there. I couldn't stand it. To this day I don't
> like being around homosexuals—in a group, that is. But
> from the first visit in a gay bar I knew I didn't want to
> spend my life hanging out as gay. The older guys were
> the most truly depressing. I didn't want to end up a tired
> old queen like that.

This was Stella's Realization: She was not homosexual; she was
a woman issued the wrong equipment. She had seen the
hopelessness of trying to live a macho life or a gay life. She
decided to visit a San Francisco psychiatrist who specialized in
transsexuals.

> I moved to San Francisco to start my new life as a woman.
> I went to a psychiatrist as the first step to getting sex
> change surgery. He went through my whole background,
> all the way back to my childhood, very thorough—it took
> nearly an hour—and he told me I wasn't gay, I was a
> transsexual.

He told me that some men who came to him just wanted hormone shots to be different and attract gay men, not really wanting to be women, but that I was a true transsexual, a woman inside.

So in less than an hour a psychiatrist had (incredibly) confirmed Stella's belief that he was "really a woman." He began that day taking the hormone shots that were the first step in changing sex, causing his breasts and hips to develop and much of his body hair to fall out.

Eventually Stella began a career as an "exotic dancer," which took her up and down both coasts of the U.S. (There is not much interest in transsexuals in the Midwest, Stella says.)

Stella's continual tugging at her bulky sweater cannot conceal a corpulent belly, her heavy makeup cannot fill her deep acne scars, her hands and feet are large, strong, mannish: She is not a beautiful woman. Her dancing career faltered when she developed a weight problem, but Stella has never regretted her decision. She is a woman.

The Case in Perspective

Stella had sufficient experience with living as a man to believe it was hopeless. She saw her future as an aging, effeminate man living a decidedly glum gay life; her vision of the future was her Realization, and she moved to assert her Self-interest. She told her family to consider her the oldest daughter in the family instead of the oldest son. She made a Clean Decision to quit being a man.

THE CASE AGAINST LAWYERS

In the ever-popular version of "true love"—the head-ringing, heart-pounding, stomach-churning-but-I-don't-need-an-Alka-Seltzer love—there is no room for the future, it is merely the happily-ever-after. So when a couple dash into a doomed relationship, refusing to heed all the danger signals, it is in the name of love.

When a man or woman runs blindly into a career, however, there is not even that wan excuse. So few people, of the many interviewed, undertook any serious investigation before entering on their careers, that it seems there must lurk in most humans some of the same instinct that causes whales to beach themselves. Earlier it was suggested that the future is not as mysterious and unpredictable as it might seem; this is especially true when you try to predict the course of a career. While it is somewhat difficult to know how far a person will rise in a given profession, it is certainly clear what each step in the rise entails and what a person's day-to-day life will be like; yet a genuine consideration of the future is often strangely absent even when one is consciously "deciding the future." The ease of entering a career, the social standing and income associated with it, seem more "real" than the expectation of what daily life will be like. A serious look at whether the career will be suitable emotionally, physically, or intellectually is frequently missing and left to be learned on the job. Stephen, the subject of this case, was one of the fortunate ones who, by chance, studied a career before entering it.

Perhaps the vast surplus of young lawyers is all Perry Mason's fault: Stephen grew up with *Perry Mason*, grew up knowing he wanted to be a lawyer; his anticipated career became a part of his self-identity even in high school. He entered a prelaw program in college and kept his grades high enough to be admitted to a number of prestigious law schools. Only then, and then almost by accident, did Stephen take a serious look at the profession for which he was so earnestly preparing. Stephen's father, a successful local entrepreneur, arranged for him to meet two lawyers who would assist him in choosing a law school and would give him some advice on picking a specialty to emphasize in school. This was to be the first time Stephen had talked to an attorney. (As Kurt Vonnegut would say, "Think about that.") Stephen did not meet Perry Mason; he did encounter his future.

Stephen described his first meeting:

> Mostly I was shocked by the confusion. There were books and papers all over. The guy, this lawyer, had to clear a stack of papers off a chair for me to sit down. He apologized for the mess by telling me how busy they had been. I asked him, "How busy are you?" He said he was

averaging sixteen hours a day. I thought he was kidding, but no shit, he meant it. And he had been doing it for over a year. I wanted to know if it was worth it. He told me how he had a new baby he barely saw and that his marriage was suffering. But, he says, it would be over in a year or two; he'd be made a partner and get some help. The help was going to be some young guy, like me, just out of law school. In the first two years the new guy "would make it or break it."

Stephen had his first exposure to the reality of life as an attorney, but he withheld judgment; after all, he reasoned, his first encounter was with a young, striving corporate attorney. His next meeting was with a lawyer who was already a partner in a prominent law firm. He recalls that meeting:

The second lawyer had an impressive office. He even had the kind of secretary you see in advertising—you know, beautiful. He offered me a drink. I said to myself, "Now, this is more like it."

Fortunately, the trappings of success did not permanently dazzle young Stephen. When the grizzled attorney realized he was sitting with a starry-eyed idealist, he explained the facts of life at the bar. Stephen recounted that conversation:

I told the second lawyer that I wanted to help defend the poor, the innocent victims of society. He told me about being a public defender. Except for the money, it didn't sound too bad, at least at first. Then he told me that nearly all my clients would be guilty. I would spend a lot of time with hostile, dirty people, many who wouldn't want anything to do with me. It would be my job to help these criminals slip through some loophole or to plea bargain them to a sentence less than the one they deserved.

This lawyer also took Stephen on a journey through other possible careers in law:

> He went on telling me about tax law and insurance law and on and on. We talked about reading and writing contracts and about studying precedents. I told him I was mostly a "people person," and he told me about personal injury and divorce cases. He kept telling me that each one was a challenging field. They were never dull, always something different to do each day. That's when *he* started talking about the long hours and the devotion to the job.
>
> I tried to imagine myself in each job, but it was hard to picture myself bouncing into the office anxious to begin each day.

So Stephen encountered his future. He was shaken by the rude fact that he would be spending long hours defending the guilty, the wealthy, and the greedy. He lost interest.

> I had always planned on law school; there was a momentum there I never much examined. Then I saw these lawyers and I started to compare their jobs to some of the jobs my friends were interviewing for. The law thing just kinda lost its momentum after that.

Stephen was slow to reveal his disenchantment, for he unconsciously knew how important law school was to his self-image. Finally he confessed his doubts to his father, who suggested that Stephen consider other careers. Only then could Stephen openly pursue alternatives. He took a job in sales and finds it well suited to his talents and personality.

The Case in Perspective

Stephen's case is another example of Futuring coming to the rescue. In effect Stephen said, "I have seen the future, and I refuse to participate." A vision of the future was Stephen's Realization. Although he had some psychological investment in the practice of law, he had not then devoted several years to law school and to starting out as an attorney, so he could painlessly experiment with an alternative career. Wisely, over the course of the next year Stephen did double-check his decision by seeking out and discussing law with other attorneys, but his decision stood—the law did not correspond to his needs.

WHEN THE GODS FALL, RUN

Quitting an important relationship is typically a result of fundamental unhappiness; the dramatic quitting cases tend to be metamorphoses from misery to harmony. What is interesting about the case of Wilson Meredith is the absence of failure: He has twice made drastic career changes, but he insists he did not dislike either abandoned career. He is simply an experimenter, a brave man willing to risk portions of his life in order to assure himself that nothing was missed. The world does not always warmly receive bold men—Wilson has been called, by friends and relatives, a "malcontent," a "fool," a "drifter," and "irresponsible." Laughing at this criticism, he labels himself a searcher. This is how he explained his self-assurance:

> Memphis, Tennessee, was my home. I grew up not knowing I was black or poor. Now, most of your people that come up from poverty live in fear of ending up back in the ghetto. But not me. I had a great life when I was poor, and if I should have to be poor again, I'll be poor again. But the funny thing is, I don't think it'll ever happen to me, because I've got several different job skills now. My contemporaries who settled into the first decent job they could get, factory work mostly, are really far more vulnerable than I am.

Wilson certainly does have diverse work skills: He had been a musician and writer, an engineer, and a lawyer, all by age thirty. Leaving his first love—writing and performing music—was the roughest decision thus far. He was performing with a group he enjoyed, he had a requited love with one of the female vocalists, the group was getting solid work and had a recording contract. The future seemed bright to everyone in and around the group, except Wilson.

> Right from the start I was bothered by the fact that I kept meeting talented performers who had put in fifteen years

and who were no further along than we were. Each time I met somebody I lumped into that category, I tried to pin down what had gone wrong. What caused them not to make it? I couldn't come up with a good reason; there wasn't one particular strand that ran through all these characters.

I shrugged off the failure of the others; things were just going too well for us. I was being creative, learning, traveling. I was saying to the world, "Watch me cook, get outa my way."

But Wilson's sense of his future plagued him. He realized that luck was more important than talent—there were more talented musicians than there were lucky ones. Musicians worried more about "contacts" than music. Writers gave away their songs in exchange for a possible break.

None of the other members of the group understood his concern; no one understood when Wilson had a mighty Realization and quit.

There was a guy who was my mentor back then. The man was a god to me. He had been in the business his whole life. He'd had a few major hits and some minor things, had scored a movie. He had the nice home, two fine cars: a real good life. And this talented, successful man was kind enough to take a young kid—I was still in college when I met him—and school him in music.

About the time I was realizing how many shady characters there were in the music industry and how much talent was going for pennies, I called my mentor, my god, for reassurance. His phone was disconnected; his house had been repossessed. Here the man was, at the top of his career, all the talent in the world, out on the street, searching for friends who would remember him. It turns out that his contact at the record company had vanished because of some scandal in the company. The people in the record company acted like the man in the scandal had never existed. And nobody wanted anything to do with my friend—he was tainted.

The downfall of his mentor was the final Realization. He decided not to pursue a goal so aleatory, a prize so evanescent.

Wilson had turned to music as a career only near the end of college; before leaving school he had turned a high math and science aptitude into an engineering degree. It was time to give his engineering knowledge a chance.

Once again he was successful; he found a good job and was well regarded. Once again he was happy in his work. Once again he quit.

After leaving a second career in four years, Wilson could be branded a quitter and a malcontent, but these labels conjure up visions of a dour, grumbling wretch. Contrast the connotations to this description of his job:

> I had no complaints. I had a lot of responsibility, a lot of projects down near the Coast, near the resorts and so forth. There was creativity in my work. I got that rush that only comes from conceiving of something, creating it, then watching it come into existence. It wasn't as much of a thrill as writing a song, but it ranked right up there. And that's what I did most of the time. Good job. No complaints at all.

If he is to be labeled, perhaps it should be the Merry Malcontent. Like so many who quit, Wilson is an adventurer, an explorer. He no more left his first two careers in anger or disappointment than Christopher Columbus left Spain in a huff. In fact, Wilson stayed an engineer until there was no adventure to be had. When did that occur? As soon as he could see his future as an engineer stretched out before him:

> Before long I had figured out just when I could expect to be a manager, a director, and so on right up to vice-president. The goal of most of us was not to screw up. We had a secure future; we just had to keep on.

His sense of the future and his restlessness increased proportionately. Finally Wilson began quietly to investigate other careers. Acknowledging the importance of legal knowledge to business success, he decided to try a year of law school as background for some entrepreneurial plans. He reveled in law school and stayed the full three years. He is now an attorney, is still happy, and is also, at least temporarily, content.

The Case in Perspective

Wilson's two quitting decisions illustrate extremes of Futuring: In his music career he felt he had insufficient control over his future; in his engineering career the future was too certain. In both decisions Wilson had his eyes on his future and his hand on the rudder of his life. He is the quintessential Man in Control.

THE RELATION OF FUTURING TO SUCCESSFUL QUITTING

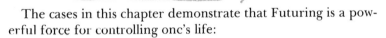

The cases in this chapter demonstrate that Futuring is a powerful force for controlling one's life:

- As the example taken from *Dubin's Lives* showed, without a sense of future there can be no control—fulfillment becomes serendipitous.

- As the case of Sylvia (the lady with the disappearing husband) verifies, a vision of the future can embolden a person to take initiatives never before considered. She gave herself written predictions of her future in order to convince herself that she could break out of poverty and dependence.

- Not only did Stella give up her male heterosexuality, she decided to give up her life as a man altogether. A recognition of a hopeless future trying to be what she was not initiated her change.

- Stephen's encounter with his future as a lawyer saved him from years of training for a job he did not want.

- Wilson demonstrated how he could be content with his life only by refusing to be content with a career that did not offer a future he truly wanted to live.

THE RULE

Each individual interviewed for this research was scored for the importance of "the future" of the existing situation in their quitting decision. The Futuring variable—the ability to foresee a relationship's future—is closely related to successful quitting.

Without a sense of future, there tends to be inaction (as in *Dubin's Lives*); nonetheless, a number of individuals reported having quit without having considered the probable future. These quits had a far lower success rate than those of the seers. Without objective consideration of the future of the existing relationship, there is a tendency for an angry outburst or a state of depression to result in the "false" Realization that the relationship is untenable. The woman who walked away from a career as a cellist and the woman who walked out on her husband after his dalliance with her friend were previous examples of basically solid relationships left impulsively because of a brief lapse. As stressed in the previous chapter on the Realization, a successful quit is a virtual certainty only when an individual has assured himself that a relationship is both deficient and also without reasonable prospects for necessary change. The latter half of this requirement, the hopelessness, is normally a result of an examination of the future.

EXCEPTIONS TO THE RULE

The Futuring variable had relatively few exceptions. The exceptions tended to be cases where the consideration of the future was not as intense as the quit was successful, rather than the more dangerous possibility, a strong sense of the future ending in an unsuccessful quit. The most engaging example of successful quitting without recognition of the future did not come from the interviews but from an autobiography called *Less Than One* by Joseph Brodsky, the Russian poet, published in *The New York Review of Books*. It is a story of growing up in the USSR.

JOSEPH BRODSKY—QUITTING WITHOUT CHANGING

Joseph Brodsky quits by instinct rather than self-analysis. Had fate been kinder to him and borne him into a country where real change, real control, were more available, he might have become an adventurer with his life, eyes on the horizon. Living in Russia, he became a drifter whose future was too unpleasant to countenance.

> Looking backward is more rewarding than its opposite. Tomorrow is just less attractive than yesterday. For some reason, the past doesn't radiate such immense monotony as the future does. Because of its plenitude, the future is propaganda. So is grass.

Without the positive force of imagining a better future, a man's life soon loses its potency.

> The trimming of the self . . . bred in us such an overpowering sense of ambivalence that in ten years we ended up with a willpower in no way superior to a seaweed's.

Although Brodsky claims to be without willpower, still he quit often. His first major quit occurred at age fifteen, when he decided to leave school. He recalls it as "not so much a conscious choice as a gut reaction." He simply "rose up in the middle of the session" and made his "melodramatic exit through the school gate," knowing he'd "never be back."

Quitting was to become a regular pattern in Brodsky's life; he learned that any desirable position in Russia was so enviable one had "to fight for that place or leave it." Brodsky's simple explanation of how he made that choice: "I happened to prefer the latter."

Such "uncontrolled" quitting is often dangerous, for a quit without active Futuring or without a Realization is usually an unsuccessful quit. Brodsky gives the impression, however, that his quitting was successful, that it at least saved him from constant fighting. Unfortunately none of his quits represented a major improvement in his life—he would insist that positive change simply was not possible in a country he views as a prison:

> The mechanism of suppression is as innate to the human psyche as the mechanism of release. Besides, to think that you are a swine is humbler and often more accurate than to perceive yourself as a fallen angel.

Thus Brodsky's story is an illustration of the role of quitting when positive change is apparently impossible; quitting becomes a mechanism for avoiding what is unpleasant. When individuals are denied a sense of alternative futures—when a better future is merely propaganda—all change becomes a gamble without losers or winners. For some, like Brodsky, the thrill of even the castrated gamble is an end in itself.

The story of Joseph Brodsky is one remarkable example of how quitting is not necessarily the result of Futuring. However, it is also an example of how, in the absence of real choices, quitting can be no more than random change.

Futuring in Perspective

As described in the previous chapter, if a Realization is to lead to a successful quit, it must normally include dual realizations— that the relationship *is not* fulfilling expectations and, that the relationship *will not* fulfill expectations. The latter obviously depends on the ability to perceive a relationship's future. The future is typically the catalyst for a strong Realization; thus Futuring and the strength of the Realization are closely related. When a realistic estimation of an undesirable future fails to bring about a Realization, it loses most of its power to stimulate positive action. Although Futuring tends to have an indirect impact on successful quitting through the Realization, it is more closely related to success than any other variable, because it also affects the other key component of quitting.

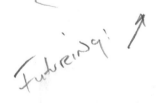

SELFISHNESS AND

SELF-INTEREST

HUNTING polar bear with dogs and sled is now rare. "Most Eskimos now use snowmobiles to run down a bear for the kill."

So says *International Wildlife* magazine. It is difficult not to be pejorative about such news, not to decry the mechanization of that which was poetic, not to whimper as another illusion falls apart . . . bang.

Naturally, if you happen to be an Eskimo dependent on the hunt for food and income, you take an opposite view. Forcing yourself and your sled dogs to the point of exhaustion chasing a vicious bear over endless miles of ice may not seem nearly as poetic as an efficiently killed bear . . . bang.

So it is with quitting—the view from within is very different than the one from afar, and practical concerns battle illusions, poetry, even morality. The greater the distance from a relationship, the easier it is to sermonize, to see what one wants to see, to say what others ought to see.

Lord Byron, prone to elegant exaggeration, looked at the sky during his first visit to Greece and commented on the beauty and portent of "twelve eagles" above the "wild pomp of mountain majesty." To his irritation, he was told they were not eagles, but Egyptian vultures. Seeing a failing relationship, it is often difficult to distinguish between the eagles and the vultures. Nowhere is the distinction more troublesome than with the thorny issue addressed in this chapter, Self-interest.

HIM OR ME

Career-quitting decisions and marriage-quitting decisions follow the same patterns, teach us the same lessons; however, the acceptability of selfishness is one point where the two seem to diverge: Individuals are expected to "maximize their self-interest" in career decisions but to be unselfish in human relations. Nonetheless, a major career change goes beyond "business," affecting one's family and friends; self-interest must often be weighed either along with or against the interests of others. Changing careers, like deciding to quit a marriage, is often distilled to the choice between staying for someone else's sake or quitting for one's own. Indeed, in a successful quit, career or marital, it is an important function of Futuring and the Realization of hopelessness to see the decision as a stark "It's him or me."

Avoiding the stark "him-or-me" situation is a Judeo-Christian tradition, for such a situation involves a moral dilemma: choosing for yourself and quitting, thus feeling guilt and perhaps being blamed by your friends; choosing the other person and staying, thus remaining in an unsatisfactory relationship and trying to be a saint by not showing resentment. The common reaction to the dilemma is to hesitate; hesitation becomes doubt, then indecision, then impasse.

No one really wants a relationship to fail. No one pursues hopelessness. Few people care to think of themselves as selfish. Choosing Self-interest and quitting is life's heart surgery. It may be needed but it's rarely wanted.

A person who has worked and struggled to make a relationship viable but who finally realizes that the future holds no hope can assert his Self-interest and quit without much fear of remorse. However, a person who asserts selfishness and quits before the opportunities to change a relationship have been exhausted—who quits, in other words, before becoming hopeless—is open to guilt and regret. Selfishness with consideration of the future is Self-interest. Selfishness without an examination of the future is merely self-indulgence.

Joseph Heller, in his novel *Good as Gold*, has this bit of dialogue, which reveals the absurdity of capricious, selfish quitting:

> "We had a perfect marriage."
> "Then why did you get a divorce?"
> "Well, Bruce, to put it plainly, I couldn't see much point in tying myself down to a middle-aged woman with four children, even though the woman was my wife and the children were my own. Can you?"

Today this character's purpose is freedom; tomorrow it could be the primacy of a solid family. Without enduring standards, it is impossible to assess self-interest accurately. Without direction in life, it is impossible to be accurately selfish, to be totally happy, to quit successfully.

UNSELFISHNESS

Unlike selfishness, Self-interest is not the opposite of unselfishness: It can be in a person's self-interest to be unselfish. For example, it is the irony of most religions that unselfishness is the key to Self-interest—be altruistic in this short life on earth and win an eternal reward greater than any possible on earth.

The results of this research suggest that once a relationship seems hopeless and is reduced to "him or me," unselfishness is not a good bet and is rarely in one's self-interest. Unselfishness is often an excuse for inaction, a justification for refusing to face feared change. The very act of weighing Self-interest is considered morally suspect and can make one feel guilty and freeze a relationship in indecision.

When "unselfishness" *is* useful is in giving "permission to leave"; many are able to quit only after assembling an artful argument that to leave a relationship is "for the good of all," "for the children's sake," or for some other rationalization (which, incidentally, is usually accurate). Once an individual has seen the future of a relationship and has realized its hopelessness, the assertion of Self-interest is the last great hurdle before a clean quitting decision can be made.

QUIT BEFORE I KILL YOU

Kathleen, known as Kat to her friends, lived in a maelstrom of a tumultuous marriage, refusing, "for the sake of the children," to quit. After eight years she was finally washed ashore, exhausted and bedraggled, with one of her children lucky to be alive.

Kat was married to an entertainer, a magician-comedian-juggler who was something of an institution at a mountain resort hotel. Her role as an entertainer's wife suited her; she considered herself an inspiration to "her man"; and was pleased to be a mother to his three children from a previous marriage. Kat, amused by her husband's rather dreamy perceptions of himself as an artist, indulged his "creative temperament." However, her acceptance began to wane after she bore their first child. Suddenly, when her husband would spend the rent money to buy her a $150 dress, it was no longer the loving gesture of a free spirit—it was just "dumb." By the time the second child arrived, it was "war."

> He always thought he was being romantic. But that's not the way you do it, because you can live without a dress or necklace, but you can't do without a place to live. And it became a routine. Then one day we get a subpoena over money he owed his ex-wife. This is in the off-season when he isn't working very much.
>
> I finally told him, "Why don't you go live with your family?" He was always talking about how much he missed his family, so I told him to go. "Bye. Go home. I don't need the aggravation." But he didn't leave.

That was the first time Kat had faced some sort of separation, but *she* didn't consider quitting; rather she tried to convince *her husband* to quit. This is a stereotypical example of an individual who fears the dislocation and guilt associated with quitting but who nonetheless seeks to end a relationship. Rather than make a tough quitting decision, she attempts to force the other person to a decision. Instead of striving to improve a relationship, such a person seeks to make it unbearable, lobbing psychological tear gas at the other half until he or she is flushed out.

Not only is this a cowardly approach, it is dicey, for in seeking to break another person, there is the possibility of violence. Further, the "smoke-'em-out" approach is typically not a conscious decision and is often implemented in anger or frustration; these are danger signals, and an *un*successful quit, with all the guilt and remorse it entails, is far more likely. Kat was unaware of the danger.

> Things got real bad, because I wasn't willing to be a doormat any longer. I started to stand up for my rights. I just wouldn't take his crap any longer.

Clearly the relationship was failing, and clearly Kat had given up trying; however, she hadn't admitted to herself she had given up . . . she hadn't had a Realization.

When a relationship is failing and one party to it completely stops trying, it would seem the end must surely be near. Not so. Thanks to a stubborn unselfishness, the entire family was to be unhappy for nearly five more years.

As the relationship deteriorated, sexual intimacy vanished. Kat is a beautiful woman, although in an unconventional way. Kat's husband was described as extremely handsome and, as a resort entertainer, was perceived to be in a position to meet available women. In short, it was the perfect culture in which to raise prodigious jealousies.

Kat tells the story of what led up to their most vicious battle:

> It had gotten to the point where I was certain that I no longer loved the man. I'm not even sure I loved him in the beginning, which sounds strange, but it happened. But being around a comedian when he's trying to write is what's strange. Here he would be, writing jokes that would make the drunks roar with laughter, but he seemed so angry when he wrote—you couldn't even get near him or he'd scream. It was like he saved all the good times in him for his audience. And when I met him, I

thought he'd be a big star in no time—I used to worry about whether he'd still love me when he was doing *The Johnny Carson Show*. Funny, huh?

The point is . . . well, I don't like to talk about it, but maybe it'll help to tell someone about it . . . what truly made me see how wrong was our being together was one Sunday afternoon when he said he was going over to my brother's house to help him do some painting. We only had one car, and I needed to do some shopping, so I told him to be back in a couple of hours. Well, he didn't come and he didn't come. I was getting suspicious 'cause my brother hadn't said anything to me about painting, and I started to think that it's real convenient that my brother didn't have a phone.

Now, I had heard rumors about my husband running around, but I hadn't listened. As my grandmother used to tell me, "Believe nothing you hear, and half of what you see." This time I couldn't help but be suspicious, so I went next door and told the neighbor this big thing about needing to borrow the car. Well, I piled the kids in and went to find him. He wasn't at my brother's, so I went to couple of places we would sometimes go. There, outside this one diner, sits our car. I go in and see this friend of ours and ask where my husband is. While the friend is stalling around, not wanting to answer, my husband walks out of the bathroom. He doesn't see me at first and goes right over to his table and sits down with these two girls: one I know and don't like. Out of the clear blue sky I walked over to him and punched him in the mouth. Right in the diner . . . zap. It took two guys to drag me out of the place.

Again Kat's instinct was to try to get her husband to quit. Standing in the diner's parking lot, she told him she wanted him to go to the other woman—"Go away, leave, get out of my life!" She said all the things a person says when they recognize failure but are incapable of initiating effectual change. Unfortunately he insisted that he was not going to leave; he got into the car with the kids and drove home. By the time Kat had returned the neighbor's car and gotten to the house, she was out of control.

> When I went inside, he was just heading up the stairs. He had made me so angry so often that I just went—well, I went wild. I grabbed him by the hair and pulled him down the stairs. We were rolling around on the floor, and he was holding me so I couldn't hit him, which just made me wilder. I kicked my way free and ran into the kitchen. He followed me. He had his fists up. I picked up a cleaver. I don't think I was intentionally going to do anything with it, I just picked it up. I just swung it. I don't think I was . . . I was just trying to scare him. I don't know. I swung it, and he got in the way. I cut open his arm, but then went right into my daughter's face. I didn't even know she was in the room; she was trying to stop him from coming at me, I guess. It cut her across her face, across one eye. Everytime I look at my beautiful little girl, I have to see that scar.

After the panic of rushing the little girl to the Emergency Room to have her face sewn back together, Kat had time to have her Realization. She couldn't help but address the future: What other horrors might be committed? At last she forsook the myths that had held her marriage together in the place of love and respect. She stopped expecting "a big break," quit believing she could just make her husband and her problems go away.

> I felt at that point if someone makes you that angry, you shouldn't be around that person anymore. If you can't solve anything without becoming so emotional, I think it's time to call it quits.

She continued to place the blame on her husband—even when she cut his arm open, she stated that he had gotten "in the way"—finally making him into such a villain in her own mind that she was ready to leave. But there was a catch—a catch that would keep her married for three more years: Three of the children were his from another marriage. She would have to abandon these three in order to leave. She perceived it as saving herself and her two children at the expense of the three left behind. It did not occur to Kat that two half families, each without the friction of hateful parents, would undoubtedly be better than they were in their present misery. It did not occur to her because she simply had no experience at making decisions. She had lived her life in the present. Plainly she did not have the skills needed to alter her life purposefully.

Instead of taking control, she turned her life over to a minister, a man who had saved her sister's marriage and was said to give salvation to troubled souls. Kat went to him so that he could make her decision; she was certain she would receive his blessing for her quit. His advice was to try again. He held Kat in his arms and prayed for her. He held her hands in his, and they cried together. Your husband loves you, he told her. (He had never met the husband.) The children need to be together. She had the power to save a family. Trust God. She relented. She didn't quit.

It is said that God works in mysterious ways. There was nothing mysterious about the way God worked when Kat simply abdicated all responsibility for the marriage, expecting God, in exchange for some Bible reading and prayer, to take over: God did nothing.

Four months later, disappointed by metaphysics, she next turned to science—a psychiatrist. That lasted two months. Through all this the relationship with her husband was still tempestuous, but not violent.

Then, slowly but inexorably, resentment came between the martyr and those she saved. Kat believed that she had stayed in a miserable marriage solely for the sake of the older children, the three who were his from a previous marriage. Having made what she considered to be a heroic stand by refusing to abandon them, she had high expectations in terms of their gratitude and cooperation. If they were ever grateful, it did not long remain uppermost in their adolescent minds. They were teen-agers who were stuck with a tense home life. Not only were they rebellious, but they began to dominate the younger children, Kat's children. Kat gradually came to associate the older children with her husband and to dislike all four.

Finally, after eight years of marriage (seven years of unhappiness), Kat turned her "unselfishness" upon her own two children; at last she was able to have an "unselfish" motivation for quitting.

> I couldn't stand to have my husband around me; I just always felt annoyed when he hung around. It was just like in school when some jerk would start hanging around you and you just couldn't stand it. Then it got to the point where I didn't like his older children. That's pretty bad. But I needed some peace of mind for me and my little ones. When they need something, I want to be able to give it to them. And I got so sick of them being bossed around by the older kids. That's all I heard about every night. You look at your kids, at these beautiful young faces, and you say, "Well, my God, I'm so worried about my life, but what kind of life do they have?" That was my main concern—them, really—not me, it was them.

Kat eventually found an apartment and, with the two younger children, moved. Life was at long last peaceful, or nearly so. The children were happy more often, and Kat was too, especially when being taken out for dinner and dancing by one of the new men she attracted. She intends to remain free; as she puts it, "I just don't think I could ever be attached to anybody anymore."

The Case in Perspective

Among cases of "attempted unselfishness," Kat's case is not, unfortunately, an anomaly. The decision to be unselfish is self-conscious—a sacrifice that certifies and makes what is being given up very vivid. The very decision process makes an abstract loss palpable; to say, "I'm going to live with this miserable man for six more years for the sake of the children," makes the daily burden heavier, not lighter. And what is the reward? An individual who chooses unhappiness for the sake of another is a hero, but only in his or her own eyes. Consciously or unconsciously this person expects to see the heroism rewarded. But the decision to stay is a decision not to change, and the relationship does not offer a hero's welcome. The burden is real, but the rewards are intangible. Unrewarded unselfishness must endure the erosion of daily annoyances. Only a saint can persevere; the nonsaints slowly turn resentful. And this resentment is on top of whatever difficulties caused a quit-or-stay decision to be needed; the relationship has renewed impetus for its downward spiral.

The nonsaint has four alternatives. First, he can redefine "unselfishness"; this is what Kat eventually did. Rather than retract her unselfishness, she merely redefined it to include quitting. Second, he can attempt to squeeze out the other party to the relationship. Kat's first instinctive attempts at a separation were to allow the marriage to be so unbearable that her husband would quit. If he had left, Kat could have been the martyr and never been forced to assert her Self-interest and act. The third alternative is to do nothing, letting the problems resolve themselves into the living of isolated lives or an "armed camp" existence. The fourth alternative is to choose one's own happiness and quit. The unselfish act, if followed by a worsened relationship, is often the motivation to declare the partner unworthy of the unselfishness. Further, the failure of unselfishness can be a new Realization that every alternative has been exhausted and the relationship is so hopeless that a clean quitting decision is then made.

MARGARET TRUDEAU: TOO HONEST OR TOO SELFISH?

Beyond Reason, the autobiography of Margaret Trudeau, received many unfavorable reviews; often the only compliment received was that it was "honest." Any book that is honest cannot be truly awful. As W. Somerset Maugham wrote, "I would sooner a writer were vulgar than mincing; for life is vulgar, and it is life he seeks." It is difficult to speak of the autobiography of any political life without muttering the words *self-serving*. Not so with Margaret Trudeau's book. It is so unequivocally candid that it is difficult not to be embarrassed for her, as if the book were a friend's betrayal of intimacies. Her story reads like the transcripts of the interviews for this research and is a relevant quitting story that illustrates the extremes to which Self-interest can be pursued.

The tragedy of physical beauty is not just that the beauty dies before its owner, but that beauty can propel a person too far too quickly. Margaret was a twenty-two-year-old "flower child" when she married the fifty-year-old prime minister of Canada. The life of a wife of a head of state seems harmless, banal. But it genuinely takes decades of tiresome training to become pristinely uneventful. Gracefully blending into the background, smiling at criticism, living under the glare of the press and the stare of bodyguards, being Caesar's wife: in short, the requirement for sharing Canada's finest public housing is shaping one's self into a living mannequin. It was too much to ask of a girl who had only six years before been in high school, thrilled to be chosen to represent her school on the Hudson Bay Company Store's teen fashion council, learning "grooming and poise and charm."

Ms. Trudeau chose a line from the Rick Nelson song "Garden Party" to summarize her later life with Pierre: "If you can't please everybody, you might as well please yourself." It is not too difficult to imagine her turning inward for direction when the press was waiting to pounce on any solecism and the security guards and her celebrity were combining to deny her privacy. Five years before she left Pierre, she had written herself a note that read, "I'm so lonely. I should be happy. I am married to a man who loves me and I have a wonderful baby. But I am terribly unhappy." Two years later—two years of trying to conform to a life she despised—she began what she called her rebellion. The rebellion consisted of becoming "a spoiled little bitch." She had failed to adapt to a life of a prime minister's wife, so she stopped trying. She refused to attend functions where her presence was expected. She had an extramarital love affair, threw temper tantrums, jetted around the world.

One of the journeys of her rebellious period was to California to attend a conference run by a guru whose most insistent insight was that "all thought leads to sorrow." Ms. Trudeau learned to feel and act rather than think. "To subjugate everything to reason and will was wrong," she concluded. "To live from moment to moment, right." The mysteries of Oriental wisdom were put to practical use: Ms. Trudeau had a philosophy to rationalize her self-indulgence.

In view of what casual "disciples" can do to distort Zen, moral laws, of which the Ten Commandments are the apotheosis, are perhaps the only way to apply philosophy to daily life successfully. The temptation to interpret philosophy in the most convenient manner is too great, particularly when the philosophy is cryptic. A vague or recondite meaning invites moral confusion. Confusion invites anarchy, and Margaret Trudeau accepted the invitation. Since she could not leave her marriage (she was not only the prime's minister's wife, she was the mother of three young children), she unconsciously sought to destroy it. She succeeded.

Ms. Trudeau nearly destroyed herself in the process; her rebellion took her to the psychiatric wing of the Montreal General Hospital suffering from severe emotional stress. When her hospitalization became widely known, she received three thousand letters, many offering the sort of advice common to those losing the battle to conform to a life for which they are ill suited or ill equipped: "Take up a hobby," said one woman. "Bake bread," said another. "Start singing," said a third. This advice is another version of the "do anything but think" strategy. Don't think. Don't recognize the hopelessness. Don't have a Realization. Don't act. Don't quit.

Margaret tried to pull her life together, to avoid thinking, but a dramatic and tragic incident forced a Realization upon her. Her dear friend and mentor Alia Hussein, wife of the king of Jordan, died in a helicopter crash. Alia had been a paragon of patience, urging Margaret by her words and her example to let things work out. In Margaret's tear-filled eyes, Alia's death made a "mockery" of that advice. It was hopeless.

Margaret moved to New York City, left not only her husband but her three children. She worked as a photographer and as an actress. For a year she experimented with various life-styles, then said good-bye to New York. She has since put together a life that she finds acceptable, and she believes that her quitting decision was correct.

Margaret Trudeau in Perspective

Ms. Trudeau ends her book by saying, "I don't, I realize, come out of the story very well. I have tried at least to be honest." Stories like hers give Self-interest a bad name. Regrettably, she failed in her relationship with Pierre, but it was her struggle to deny failure that made her become self-indulgent, selfish, destructive. If she had earlier addressed the future and asserted her Self-interest, the emotional collapse and the pain she selfishly inflicted on her family could have been avoided.

"All thought leads to sorrow," she had heard and believed. Some thought, some planning, some thoughtfulness could have avoided much sorrow.

SELF-HEROISM

For over seven years he was Father Tim. Today he is simply Mr. Kelly, the guy to see if you want a loan from the First National Bank. M-G-M would not have had him as a Catholic priest: His eyes never twinkle or crinkle, he has neither an accent nor a lilt to his voice, he looks, in fact, very much like a banker. Yet he was a priest and would still be one today if the Church permitted priests to marry.

Even before Tim finished seminary he had been tempted by a woman who was preparing to become a nun. Both felt their relationship was somewhat dicey and a little risqué, although Tim's description reveals only the most innocent of times:

> We would meet for a cup of coffee, and you know, chat a little. That was it, a platonic relationship. Then, after she entered the convent, she wrote me a little. It was at least somebody I could share with, express myself about what was going on in my life, and so on. It was a very strong platonic relationship, a genuine friendship.

This was Tim's first close adult relationship with a woman. Both he and the nun were guarded, defensive; both had been warned about the irresistible magnetic attraction of human sexuality and neither party wanted to risk the possibility of being galvanized into unbridled sexual congress.

I developed a crush on her, and she saw what was coming and placed some distance between us. She didn't want to get away from me—she valued the friendship for all the same reasons I did—but she withdrew in order to keep things from becoming too emotional. She was always aware of maintaining our virginal and celibate distance. Eventually, there was some hurt involved in the relationship—I hurt her and she hurt me. It made me wonder about the priesthood—not that I thought of leaving the priesthood—it just made me wonder about the obstacles to having a female friend. A friend was such a marvelous discovery for me. And she was an attractive gal. I discovered I was attractive to an attractive gal.

The obstacles to female friendship were, Tim realized, designed to be prophylactic, to forestall even the possibility of a temptation. It succeeded, but only temporarily; both Tim and his nun parted (although both eventually left the Church and both married).

For years after his platonic fling, Tim, settled into a teaching position associated with a metropolitan cathedral, ignored his sense of knowing part of what he was missing and imagining the rest. Then there was Jan. In Tim's words he had always entertained "serious thoughts" about leaving the priesthood, but now he had "serious challenges."

All of us think about alternatives, but for the first time I had someone who drew me to the brink of a decision. For the first time I was in a relationship that was evolving, on its own, without anyone fighting it. We developed a mutual dependence. It wasn't physical—more an affectionate friendship—but naturally the relationship sought to define itself. What were the limits to be?

It was Tim's turn to put some distance in the relationship. He felt the momentum and was troubled; he was, after all, the son of Irish Catholic parents, the counselor of dozens of troubled children, and still emphatically a believer. Some experimenting with female friendship was an adventure, but his vows were sacred. When he realized that there would soon be a choice of Jan or the priesthood, he fled. He requested a teaching position in the Orient. When his religious superior learned the motivation for Tim's request, a reassignment for one year was pushed through. Tim simply informed Jan that he had to leave. The relationship was not ended, however; Tim was just testing.

I think now that my decision to go to Japan was not a decision to leave Jan. It might have been another way of procrastinating; it might have been another way of running away from an immediate decision. It was a way of gaining distance. I never pictured my friendship . . . never wanted my friendship . . . to be entirely cut off. I knew that if I was going to make a decision, I had to be fair. I wanted to be fair to the families involved at the Catholic school, to the students and all. All these people looked up to me as a priest. They looked up to me as a celibate priest.

Although Tim said that he was going to Japan to forget, his absence had the serendipitous effect of separating him from those who might have their faith injured by losing their priest to marriage. Instead of clearing his mind, he was clearing his conscience. Still, the decision was not easy.

I was going through the torment of decision. I was spending a lot of time in prayer. I was taking counsel. And the whole time I was keeping up a correspondence with Jan. Finally, after many months, I wrote her a letter saying that I was staying in the ministry. My letter crossed a letter of hers that basically said, "If you're having such a tough time deciding, let's forget it."

Then I spent the rest of the year protesting how peaceful I was. Beware the man that protesteth too much. But I kept insisting to myself that I was doing the right thing. I was trying to talk myself into wanting what I told myself I ought to want. My family is so devout. I have a lot of friends. I have played a great part in a lot of people's lives. I was Father Tim this and Father Tim that. There's a certain clerical status you have, and a social status too. Plus there is a strong feeling of fraternity within the religious order I was in. Plus the burden the Church puts on you as far as the fidelity business, and the guilt. My conclusion was to return to the U.S. and give myself one hundred percent to Him, to a celibate ministry.

Tim returned to visit his superior for reassignment. Tim wanted his old position back; he knew it to be available. His superior told him no, he was being sent to a different city, a different state, so that he would be "away from this woman." Tim dwelled on that remark, building grave resentment for the "paternalistic attitude" and the "Scarlet Letter" innuendo. He never doubted that he would see Jan again. If seeing her drove him from the priesthood, he should not be a priest, he concluded.

When Tim went to Jan, he knew that all his "protesting" was a facade. Within a week he had let it slip to Jan that he was once again reconsidering his vows. She said simply, "I don't want to go through that again."

Tim knew then he had to make a decision. He had carefully set the stage. Having gone to Japan, he could tell himself and his family and friends how much he had tried everything to escape a love bigger than he. That year in the Orient had also broken the dependence on him that he felt dozens of families had: He could leave the priesthood now without a scene. Finally he felt that he was in a position to be allowed to be laicized—permitted to step down from the priesthood without being excommunicated. Still, there was the guilt. Tim felt selfish. Sure, his quitting would be a benefit to Jan and her children, but he was dedicated to being selfless and he could not force himself to evaluate his Self-interest coolly—not until a vision of the future came to the rescue. As Tim struggled anew with his decision, he stopped to picture his life in the priesthood should he not marry Jan. He had often pictured his life with Jan, had cherished the imaginings, but never had examined the other path. When he did, he had his final Realization. What he saw was a broken, bitter man. He saw himself in the priesthood as "a cripple" who, without Jan or someone like her, would turn to other comforts, probably seeking solace in the bottle more often than in the Bible. What use could he be to others? Who would benefit from his destroying himself?

In this way Tim resolved his selfishness; if he stayed in the priesthood, he would not be a benefit to the Church. Only by leaving the priesthood could he bring joy to Jan and her children, and only by leaving could he save himself. Tim had made his decision to leave an indirect benefit to the Church. It wasn't selfish to save Father Tim from alcoholism and bitterness; it was heroic. Tim had finally succeeded in convincing himself that his quitting was unselfish, although it was in his Self-interest.

Tim married Jan and has "grown considerably." His adjustment was smooth, and he has no regrets. He has remained a devout Catholic active "in the life of the Church."

The Case in Perspective

Tim's story is a dramatic example of the role of selfishness and self-interest in a career-quitting decision. As in most successful quits, Tim needed the reassurance of hopelessness; he convinced himself—and who else matters?—that he was not capable of living without Jan. This Realization came about only when he looked to the future and saw his destruction. Quit or be destroyed, he was able to tell himself. Save yourself or you'll never be of use to anyone. Only then could he feel certain that anyone, even Jesus, would forgive him for leaving the priesthood.

CURTAINS FOR SELFISHNESS

While Father Tim is an unlikely man for Hollywood to cast in the role of a priest, Allison could play no role but that of an actress—she was quintessential theater. Tall, glamorous but unspoiled, she energetically pursued an acting career.

> I was studying acting and taking dancing, yoga, and fencing lessons. I was connected with two local theaters and tried to go to at least two auditions a week, mostly for commercials but also for movie roles. Unfortunately, I pushed myself a little too hard. I only slept five hours a

night and had to keep my weight down about fifteen
pounds below what I was meant to weigh to keep my
cheeks from ballooning up—my face cheeks, not the
other ones, although they were naughty at times too.

Allison was subject to dizzy spells and to infections. The
former took her to an internist, the latter to a gynecologist.

The most incredible thing happened, both these doctors I
was visiting showed a lot of interest in me. Well, on the
one hand, I didn't have any time for social life at that
point, but on the other hand I was visiting these doctors
because I was so overexerted. I decided to take a month
off and just say the hell with it and live a truly, marvel-
ously debauched life. I started going out with both of
them. One was married, I soon found out, but I didn't
care. I was determined to be shameless and just get it all
out. Maybe it was get it all in. Anyway, I hardly got out of
bed for a whole month. I mean that literally. The one guy
loved to cook me dinner and serve me in bed. It was like
Tom Jones every night.

Allison was reacting to the strain of her ambitious self-
improvement program. Her previous self-discipline was
matched in intensity by her newfound license. She grew restless
as her appetite for the capricious became sated; this was a lady
who needed a challenge and who needed income.

When I went back to my classes and auditions, I just
didn't have so many nights for my dalliances, so I told
both my lovers to back off a little. The one cried when I
told him—he thought I had found another man. He had
never guessed where I learned so much about gynecol-
ogy. That's acting. Both of them offered to support me,
although the married one was growing very fidgety about
our affair. I could tell he was starting to get a whole guilt
trip, so I eased myself out of that one. I do still get free
medical care from him.

Having tasted laziness and indulgence, Allison was never the
same. Shortly after accepting the use of a friend's oceanside

condominium in which to live, she acknowledged that the momentum was being drained from her career; she needed an ascetic life in order to avoid temptation. With unconditional determination she resumed her monomaniacal pursuit of excellence in her craft. She was never certain how close she came to her ill-defined goal of excellence, but by the concrete, albeit philistine, measure of income, she was a success.

> No, I wasn't really a star. I was getting some good parts in some bad movies and a good bit of commercial work. I was making a bunch of money, although I was afraid of it. I just kept myself buried in my work. I was still seeing the one doctor socially, the other one professionally. I permitted myself to have one night a week to go out, and maybe one social-type lunch a week. That was plenty. With my career going so well, I had everything I wanted, except, of course, the chance to get some of those really choice roles on the big-budget films, but I knew my chance would come. When I did my yoga exercises, I would tell myself I was a bubble rising to the surface. Nothing could stop me, I was on my way to the surface. Rising. Rising. Rising.

Allison was right about rising, but wrong that nothing could stop her. Three events, all in the space of six weeks, stood her world on its head; her bubble was headed to the bottom.

> It was the most amazing six weeks I've ever heard of. First, I finally got a big, big part—a major-studio film that would have all the money behind it and the names to draw the crowds. It was ecstasy. Glorious. I went out two nights in a row to celebrate. But . . . but, but, but . . . I was feeling unhealthy. My boyfriend, the internist, examined me and ran all those painful and/or embarrassing tests. He told me I was pregnant. Pregnant! I didn't believe him and went to my old friend the gynecologist. Pregnant. I was catatonic. The internist insists I marry him and have the baby. He tells me he'll kill me and then himself if I kill our little baby. Then a week later, when I'm still trying to make up my mind, he had a heart attack.

The internist let Allison assume the responsibility for his hospitalization. She added it to the guilt she already felt about the planned abortion. She was faced with stopping a child's birth and breaking apart the man she loved in order to pursue her career.

> I fell ill again, strung out over the monumental proportions of the decisions. I was very much into letting my inner self become free at the time. I did not philosophically accept the notion of guilt, yet the decision kept coming down to two against one—the baby and my husband-to-be against me. My indecision became a decision. I decided to let go and see what life gave me instead of trying to always force myself to be something I had previously intellectualized.

Allison was emotionally exhausted and physically near collapse. Her decision was to give in. As happens so often, "unselfishness" is simply easier than its alternatives.

Having made her decision, Allison was ready to embrace her new role immoderately as wife and mother. Playing on her singleness of purpose, her new husband convinced her to take five years off and devote those years to bearing and raising two or three children through their critical first years. There would be plenty of time for acting, he reassured her. She agreed to quit.

> It was nearly ten years ago I decided to leave my career for five years. You can't go home. It's not just that the contacts grow cold and distant and you have to start at the bottom again; it's that you lose the zeal. My drama coach used to tell me I had "fire in my belly" . . . now I have stretch marks. My confidence is gone. I see all the young women who are free to devote themselves heart, mind, and soul to acting. Acting is not just their life, it's who they are, it's their self-image. After nine years of hiring and firing maids and attending to the PTA, I think of myself as a housewife. And to think of yourself as a housewife is to think of yourself as useless. I'm an assistant to three children, an accessory to the crime of raising three spoiled brats. So to try to pull this body back to the point of being an instrument of emotions is not just the task of overcom-

ing nine years of rust; it's a task of doing it while being a mother and wife. I'm too intimidated to try. When I was young, I climbed the mountain before I knew how dangerous it was. Now I know too much.

The Case in Perspective

There are a great many excuses for failing to change, for refusing a bold move like quitting even when the future is hopeless. Of the great excuses, the greatest is "I did it for them." Unselfishness is the grand excuse for refusing to succeed.

But Allison's case is quite the opposite: She chose to be unselfish. Naturally—human naturally—Allison often regrets her decision. In successful quits, the vision of the future leads to a sense of hopelessness for the relationship; the very vision serves as a continuing reminder that the correct decision was made. For Allison the future held great hope, endless promise. She saw some other actress find fame in the role she could have had. She had to watch as someone else lived her glamorous future.

Allison has neither a vision of hopelessness nor a Realization to sustain her. Instead she has her husband and children. She loves her family but not her life. She is not a saint, is not above being resentful when her life as a doctor's wife is dull or frustrating. In retrospect she acknowledges that she made the wrong decision to leave her career. She failed to examine enough options; if she had it to do over, she would have the baby but take off five weeks instead of five years. She would remain single, either giving the baby to the father or asking for enough financial support to hire a nanny. Only after securing her success would she take time off for a family. To have a wholly unconditional love for family, that family must be planned selfinterestedly. Spare the children unselfish births.

JOHN DEAN—THE WATERGATE QUITTER

Of the five White House figures most closely associated with the sludge called Watergate—Nixon, Haldeman, Ehrlichman, Mitchell, and Dean—only John Dean truly made a decision to quit. The others resigned in name only, forced from their positions. Ironically, of the five, only John Dean was fired. A combination of Futuring and Self-interest was responsible for Dean's ability to escape the conspiracy to make him the "fall guy" for Watergate.

The chill that comes from *Blind Ambition*, Dean's story of his Watergate experience, is in realizing how far he slid into the Watergate cover-up without a decision to be involved. Following orders and assisting his associates and superiors, he gave away his integrity piecemeal; only when it was all but gone did he recognize his loss. As so often happens, a pencil and paper changed a life: Dean did not become convinced of his own culpability until he tried to put the fact on paper. Endeavoring to compose a report to President Nixon on the cover-up, he was compelled to put his involvement on paper. Recognizing the power of certainty that comes from having committed his misdeeds to paper and knowing that his report could be used against him as a "confession," he acknowledged to himself for the first time that he needed to be calculating in his actions. Dean contemplated consulting a criminal attorney to assay his liability, not an easy decision. In *Blind Ambition* Dean explained:

> As usual, I felt exhausted when I arose the next morning. While showering, I thought again about hiring a criminal lawyer. If I hired a lawyer for myself, went to the prosecutors and told them everything I knew—except about the President—I'd really be dumping on Mitchell and Haldeman. I didn't give a damn about Ehrlichman, but for me I'd be a squealer, and just to save myself.

So Dean confronted his own selfishness. But with some skillful rationalization Dean hit upon a way to seek the counsel of a criminal attorney without being selfish: He would seek an assessment of the liability of all those involved, not just his own. He would be performing a service. Dean's compromise plan encountered a setback even before it could be implemented: John Mitchell chose to confide in Dean that he (Mitchell) had approved the "Liddy Plan" (a list of sordid, stupid "campaign intelligence" activities).

Mitchell was in trouble and needed help. He had just

SELFISHNESS AND SELF-INTEREST   [97]

> trusted me with his biggest secret, and if I told the truth I
> would have to betray this one too—Deep down I knew
> Mitchell had played his best card. He was counting on my
> feeling for him, laying himself in my hands. . . . Now I felt
> the razor edge between the squealer and the perjurer, I
> had never felt more squalid.

Dean eventually did choose to visit a criminal lawyer for advice, knowing that his conversation would benefit from the attorney-client privilege. Attorney Charles Shaffer gave it to Dean straight and hard, telling him that only with luck and "the right moves" could Dean hope to stay out of jail and save his license to practice law. It was Shaffer who pushed Dean to offer his story to the Watergate prosecutors despite Dean's reluctance—his loyalty to Mitchell, Haldeman, and Nixon. In this brutal, coarse exchange Shaffer convinced Dean to break the cover-up:

> "You don't know," Charlie said condescendingly. "Maybe
> you can stay out of the cover-up. Frankly, I don't give a
> damn. It's your ass or theirs. Whose do you want to save?"
>   "Mine, of course, but . . ."
>   "Do you think they're going to protect you when the
> shit hits the fan?"
>   "No, but I know damn well they won't if they think I
> stuck the knife in them when I didn't have to."
>   "You have to, unless you want to keep lying and covering up. You want to do that?"
>   "No."
>   "Are you ready to meet with the prosecutor?"
>   "Yes."

Having seen his likely future—prison, getting drummed from his profession, being labeled as the Watergate villain—and having chosen Self-interest, Dean quit the cover-up and, in effect, quit the White House.

John Dean in Perspective

By the time John Dean realized how far he had sunk in the

mire of Watergate, he had no desirable options and but one major decision—to remain loyal or quit, to decide between Self-interest and the selfish interest of a president and his staff. Living in the future until he was exhausted and ill, Dean failed to devise a plan to remain loyal without sacrificing himself to an unworthy cause. His future as a loyal White House staffer was hopeless; he sought the only alternative he had, to ask the prosecutors and the public for a better future than the White House would offer. Apparently he received it. Although his attorney could not keep him out of prison or in the bar, Dean served a fairly light prison term. Although there was no way for him to surface from Watergate as a hero, he was in many ways vindicated. He was given celebrity without extreme animus. John Dean will never be called a team player, but he quit a losing team.

THE RELATION OF SELF-INTEREST TO SUCCESSFUL QUITTING

The most painful moment in a quitting decision is when it is reduced to him-or-me. It is the instant when a future of unrelenting dissatisfaction must be weighted against the agony of leaving someone who doesn't want to be left. Bear a dull pain or inflict a sharp one. This rankles, grates, hurts. The decision to quit is often a decision to pose for a portrait of a self-centered person, a hurter, a bastard, a quitter. Still, as the cases in this chapter have shown, the assertion of Self-interest is an important step toward freedom.

- Kat, the wife of the comedian, tried so hard to be unselfish that she nearly killed her daughter. The preservation of her self-image as an unselfish mother cost her and her children several years of happiness.

- Margaret Trudeau overcame seemingly irresistible pressures in order to free herself from a life she despised. She is an illustration of Self-Interest that, in the long run, tends to be in the interest of all.

- Father Tim saved himself. He would not have survived

in the priesthood, but he asserted his Self-interest and quit before he needed to prove his destruction.

- Allison gave up her acting career for her family. She then had only part of herself to give to her family—she left much of her heart, energy, and commitment in the theater.

- John Dean left the "team" rather than play the position chosen for him, that of villain.

THE RULE

Self-interest is present in each life decision. What makes it so problematical in the quitting situation is that it can negatively affect important people in one's life. Often the decision can be reduced to a choice between staying for the sake of those important people or quitting for one's own sake. The results of this research indicate that the gesture of staying in a relationship for unselfish reasons is usually doomed to fail. Unselfishness in a relationship does not demand too much, but the demands are for too long. Sustained unselfishness requires uncommon saintliness.

True unselfishness should not be confused with rationalizing Self-interest into an "unselfish" act. As long as the potential quitter is pursuing his own interests, the more individuals that can be pulled into the category of those who are helped the better. If the quitter can call his motives unselfish even as he pursues his own interests, he is even more likely to succeed.

A successful quit thus need not be "selfish," in the sense of being inconsiderate of the interests of others, for others are often benefited by the decision to quit. However, unless the quit is a part of choosing the most desirable course for an individual's own life, the quit is unlikely to be successful.

EXCEPTIONS TO THE RULE

Self-interest has a complex relationship to successful quitting. While the assertion of Self-interest is normally a necessary ingredient in a successful quit, Self-interest is rather ubiquitous in that it seems also to appear in many unsuccessful quits. The distinction between selfishness and Self-interest becomes crucial to understanding how a seemingly vehement assertion of Self-interest may simply be an outburst of indulgence rather than a self-interested choice of futures.

BLIND SELFISHNESS

They were high school sweethearts: Derek loves Tina. They were "pinned" in college, so inseparable that friends called them "Derna." Perhaps they were too close, for soon after they were engaged, Derek grew complacent about Tina's love, rarely noticing her beauty, support, and friendship.

During his senior year at the University of Texas, Derek began the thrilling, humiliating experience of searching for a job after graduation. He looked first in Dallas, but the job market was unfavorable. Salaries were higher in other less desirable cities, and companies in other cities actually wanted to talk to him, whereas in Dallas he had to wheedle an unpromising interview. Derek describes his decision to leave Dallas:

> Dallas is an executive city when it comes to engineers, not the place for a guy fresh out of school to start. You take a cut in salary to work in there, if you even can find something. In a way, I wanted to leave Texas. When I got out of high school, I thought I cut the cord with my parents, but I knew I really wasn't on my own. I'd lived my twenty-two years in the same area. My parents were there, my girl friend was there, and her parents were there. It was time to go. I ended up taking a job in Birmingham.

Derek made his decision to leave Dallas without consulting his parents, friends, even Tina. His decision was a defiant act of independence and a statement of freedom. Derek describes telling Tina of his decision:

> I kinda used to run things in our relationship, so I just laid it out for her—what the job market was like and how I felt and that there simply was a ninety-nine-percent chance that I'd be leaving. After telling me she was happy for me to have the new job and all, she worked around to

asking me about her role in all of this. I talked around it, and then she just came out and said, "What about marriage?" I had to expect it would come up, but I was still a little dazed and just babbled, "But . . . well, you know . . . I don't know"—just saying nothing. I avoided the issue.

Surely Tina was hurt by Derek's sudden avoidance and his new independence. Rather than question Derek's decision, she found her own out-of-town job offer. She told Derek of her new alternative late one afternoon as the two strolled along a golf course. She told Derek that she had to let her potential employer know the following week if she would be taking the job. Are we, she asked Derek, going to be married or not? Derek recalls his answer:

> There are a number of things I want to do before I get tied down, things I don't want to have the consent of a wife to do. I want to get my own apartment, pick out my own furniture without having someone over my shoulder saying, "No, I don't like it." Any mistakes will be my own mistakes. A new job is a lot of stress and extra pressure, and I don't want to try to do two major things at once. I want to buy my own car without Dad being there while I'm dickering with the guy. Things like that.

Tina kept her composure. As Derek described her, "She kept a stiff upper lip." Derek went on to tell her that he was also thinking of her, letting her do some experimenting, freeing her to take a coveted job offer in Florida. They briefly discussed the possibility of living together without marrying; however, Tina was "the basic Southern girl with virtues and things of that nature," her parents were "definitely of the old school" and her father was "a very large man with a huge temper," so the idea was rejected. Tina proposed instead that she find a job in Birmingham and find a separate apartment in the same city. Derek finally confessed that he "just didn't want to be bothered with having to worry about her." Finally she understood—Derek wanted to be on his own, free to be selfish. Tina accepted the Florida job offer and moved on the day after graduation. A month later Derek moved to Alabama and discovered that he had not given any hard thought to life in a new city or to life without Tina.

It was an awkward situation. It was hard to get back into the swing of things, having to start messing with girls again. I had to go to parties hoping to meet some people and go out drinking and partying and the like. I even went to discos. It's hard getting back into shape again. It's kind of uncomfortable. It's disheartening when you start losing your touch—growing old or something like that.

I wished it hadn't worked out the way it did. I guess I wanted to have my cake and eat it too. I should have looked more in Dallas or had Tina move to Alabama. She went off to Florida and jumped right into things. I try to call her but she's never home. The last time I got a hold of her, there was some guy there. I didn't blame him for being there—she's a perfect girl.

Derek was selfish. He was indulgent, impulsive, and inconsiderate. The quit occurred before the relationship was hopelessly unsatisfactory, without a Realization or a vision of the future. Derek did not stop to evaluate his Self-interest, failed to see the future he was choosing. Just as false Realizations can accompany an outburst of anger, so are there bursts of selfishness that are not necessarily related to Self-interest. An impulsive quit, whether it is the result of anger or selfishness, is far less likely to be successful than a quiet acceptance of hopelessness followed by a determined, but not hostile, assertion of Self-interest.

Self-interest in Perspective

While Self-interest is typically a necessary ingredient in a successful quit, it is the *interaction* of the Realization and Futuring with Self-interest that distinguishes the cases of those who made a correct decision when asserting their Self-interest. Self-interest does not stand on its own as one of the key components of a successful quit. *Un*selfishness, however, is a common reason for not quitting and can be a reason for quitting. As the preceding cases show, unselfishness is dangerous, usually leading to an incorrect quitting decision.

THE IMMACULATE

DECISION—MAKING A

CLEAN QUITTING

DECISION

PART of growing up in America is being told what you are.

You are what you eat.
You are what you think.
You are what you read.
And so forth.*

There comes a dramatic moment in most successful quits when individuals know that they will leave a relationship. At that moment, people discover what they are *not*. If the decision is a Clean Decision, a person can conclude, *You are not what you quit.* This is the power of negative thinking. After weeks, months, or years of agonizing, of trying to salvage an unsatisfactory relationship, of finally giving up and acknowledging a hopeless future, of finally asserting Self-Interest, and then . . . and then . . .

In fact, a mildly amusing parlor game is to go around the room making up these tawdy profundities. You are what you see. You are what your friends see. You are what you are. The game ends only when someone quits. A side benefit of this game is to make all participants grateful to the quitter, an important lesson.

finally, one redefines a life. In an instant a person is no longer
part of a failed relationship, no longer unhappily married, no
longer someone who hates his or her work, no longer what one
has quit.

A common element in the histories of most successful quits is a
clear recollection of the moment of the decision to quit. The
arrival of the decision is often described as being nearly mystical:
"After weeks of worrying, I woke up one morning and just knew
I would leave," or "I had tried for months to make a decision,
then suddenly I knew, down deep in my heart, I would quit."
This is the Clean Decision: It is as if the conscious mind had
argued both sides of the quitting case, then left the issue for the
subconscious to decide. One never knows how long this jury of
the subconscious will be out, or if it will ever reach a decision, but
if and when it does, the verdict is announced suddenly but
quietly, usually during sleep or in a state of daydreaming relaxa-
tion. The decision is final, irrevocable.

The analogy of a verdict from the subconscious describes the
perfectly Clean Decision. As the cases in this chapter will illustrate, there are graduated degrees of cleanness that fall short of
a sudden steeling of conviction but nonetheless are on the same
continuum. The further along that continuum the quitting decision is, the greater the likelihood of a successful quit.

The Clean Decision is not to be confused with a "clean break"
or another dramatic exit from a relationship; the Clean Decision
is solely a mental process, not the physical act of leaving. Clean
Decisions are made as long as half a lifetime before an individual
actually closes the door on a relationship and walks away. The
Clean Decision is the commitment to act, not the act itself. A
clear-cut decision to quit may seem to be associated with an easy,
one-sided decision: The easier the decision, the more certain the
quitter and thus the less the likelihood of regret. This is *not* the
essence of the Clean Decision; the ultimate Clean Decision, the
subconscious verdict, is most associated with agonizing, compli-
cated quitting decisions, not obvious ones. The Clean Decision is
a deep certitude that ends the struggle to decide. The greater
the struggle, the more peaceful the victor.

The Clean Decision is then neither the act of quitting nor the
fact of having faced an easy decision. It is also not a Realization.

A Realization is a discovery that the relationship is and will be unsatisfactory, a decision that the relationship has failed one's expectations. The Realization usually causes despair, fantasies of escape, and final desperate attempts at changing the relationship; next comes the assertion of Self-interest, and finally the decision to quit. The Realization and Clean Decision can occur virtually simultaneously or be separated by months or years of mental turmoil. Typically, several months elapse between the discovery of hopelessness and the decision to depart.

As the cases that follow will show, the Clean Decision is a victory over inertia, a willingness to take control of one's life. Futuring, Realization, and Self-interest combine and await the Clean Decision; they are the thorny bush on which the rose blooms. After the decision must come the often sad task of implementation, of physically quitting, but a Clean Decision provides the reserve of quiet strength necessary for success.

NOT FOR GOD'S SAKE

Of all the quitting situations studied as part of this research, the longest separation between the decision to quit and the actual quit occurred in Mary's case—eight and a half years passed between her Clean Decision and her leaving her troubled marriage.

Mary was wed early in college to an "older man" of twenty-nine. Although taciturn and diffident by nature, Mary grudgingly took a leadership role in her marriage:

> Maybe I fell for him because he was older and I really wanted to be taken care of. But it turned out just the other way around. He acted like after the wedding was all over, he could stop trying. He took a lesser job that was shorter hours and less money and started drinking more. Since I was in college and he wasn't making very much, we ended up living with his parents. Then he started drinking even more and working even less.
>
> I'm not the type to yell and scream and bitch, so I just tried to accept him. And then he started staying out late, sometimes overnight. He told me he needed some time to be with the guys, and I still believe that's all there was to it

. . . that, and that he wanted to get away from the house; we had his parents always there, and by then we had our daughter.

Mary was soon attempting to change her husband rather than change herself. She claims that she was patient and understanding, but insistent—she had goals in her life that would never be met if her husband was not more aggressive.

Our [physical] living conditions improved overnight when his parents bought us a small house to live in. I guess they were politely pitching us out, but we had a free house to ourselves. Once we did, he couldn't use the house for an excuse anymore. We had problems and we both knew it.

If Mary's husband knew of the problems, he certainly was more inclined to escape than resolve them. He went out more often and came home drunk every time. Mary could not envision a happy life with her husband.

Our daughter was just a few months old when I decided to map out my life. I'm a big dreamer, I guess. I knew that I could get a government job and I decided that I wanted that security. I also decided to move from our small town to a large city where there was industry and lots of new people.

I knew then that my husband didn't fit into the plans, but I decided that I'd find some way to work things out. I guess I just couldn't fit him into my dreams.

Mary had her Futuring and her Realization, but she had several major obstacles to deciding to quit and implementing a decision: She was a devout Southern Baptist in a wildly conservative small-town church, so divorce was immoral, and selfish needs irrelevant; she had a baby only three months old; she had no work experience; her husband was psychologically dependent on her. Yet, in the face of these obstacles, and before knowing how she would surmount each one, she asserted her Self-interest and made a Clean Decision to quit.

After a year and a half of marriage, I was sitting home alone, holding our baby daugher, daydreaming. I was only happy with our marriage for the first couple of months at the most, and our problems were on my mind a lot. I had already done the mapping out of my life, but I had no idea where to start. That made me sad. I was still in college and I needed to work on a term paper, but I just couldn't do anything but sit in our rocking chair, holding my tiny little daughter. I was alone with my baby and I just said to her, "Don't worry, your mother is gonna make good. Your father isn't . . . but don't worry, your mother is gonna make good." That was it. I knew. That was my decision to leave him, and I never again doubted it.

That decision was so complete, so irreversible, that it carried Mary through eight and a half years of preparations. Because she felt her husband was a loving father and not overly painful to live with, she took her time; she finished school, got some work experience, and allowed their daughter to grow older.

We were married, and it was all right, but the main reason I was able to be patient with him was that I knew it wasn't forever. I still had my plan to move to a city and start over, which I didn't want to do until I was ready.

Their tenth wedding anniversary approached. Mary was ready. Anticipating leaving caused her to become ill. She lost thirty pounds; still, she continued her preparations. The first major step was to reassert her Self-interest. She decided to leave her Church. Blaming her illness, she skipped services and resigned from teaching Baptist Sunday school and from the Visitation Committee.

I stopped church point-blank, everything. I felt I was forced to choose between the Church and divorce. I refused to see the reactions to my divorce on the faces of the church people and have all the guilt feelings. I decided to leave rather than face it. Now I think it was a mistake, because I needed God at that time of the divorce more than any time in my life.

(The decision to quit her church is a little quitting story inside a quitting story. Mary did not experience any hopelessness in her relation to her church, nor did she explore other options; her assertion of Self-interest was premature. Predictably, it was not a successful quit.)

> I decided, hey, I better get everything in order instead of lying around being sick. I divided the furniture, took what I thought was fair. I gave him the house, since it was from his parents and he needed the security more than I did. I started looking at apartments and shopping for furniture. Once I got busy, I wasn't sick.

No longer ill, but still very scared and feeling very alone, Mary moved into a new apartment in the same town. Her husband was never sure what had happened, why Mary had suddenly up and left; he had no idea that Mary's daydreams of departure had sustained her for over eight years.

Mary eventually moved to a new city, made new friends, got the government job she wanted, and now feels happier than at any other time in her life. She grew so independent that she freed her husband from the child support ordered by the court. But Mary has also freed herself; she is in control.

The Case in Perspective

The only regret Mary has about her quitting decision is that she waited so long to implement it. One power of a Clean Decision is to provide a blanket of peace, the result of a redefinition of the relationship. This redefinition can enable a person to forestall the act of quitting for months or years—sometimes too long. It took a realization of the passage of time (the approach of the tenth anniversary) for Mary to have the catalyst she needed for the implementation of her plan.

OUT OF THE FAMILY

The typical response to marital conflict is avoidance—increased defensiveness and greater psychological distance. Emotional retreat is even, on occasion, a successful strategic maneuver, allowing sufficient safe time for a crisis to pass, the marital climate to change. A failing relationship between mother and child is more difficult to correct than between husband and wife: How can a child be avoided without also killing any hope for improvement? Moreover, how do you quit a child? Quitting a dependent child is like quitting yourself: There seems to be no convincing, acceptable way to say good-bye. In the place of quitting is the knowledge that the child will eventually become an adult and depart; however, the younger the child, the more distant the departure.

Emma had a daughter, her second child, whom she could not control or help. She describes the relationship:

> By her early teens, Brooke was quite removed. As she grew older, she became more and more involved in her schizophrenia. The worst part was that she would disappear; she'd just lose herself, literally not knowing where she was. She would also fantasize; I was never sure whether the stories she told were actually things happening to her or just her imagination. I was constantly trying to compensate for her. I guess I would overcompensate. She was so miserable, so unhappy, I was trying to bend over backward to make life easier for her.
>
> Brooke was in therapy, but the problems persisted. Paying for a psychiatrist was money spent in vain, but what choice was there? The psychiatrist scared Brooke, because she began to understand she had real problems and she feared being put away, being locked up, caged. Once she turned violent, and we had to have her briefly committed to a hospital. But we couldn't just send her away. We didn't have the money or the heart.

The relationship deteriorated steadily. Emma's attempts to "compensate" seemed only to worsen Brooke's behavior. Emma held on, knowing that she had only three years until her daughter would be eighteen and allowed to try life on her own. But Emma's strength eroded as her other children and her husband felt the impact of Brooke's behavior; the family was disintegrating before Emma's eyes. Emma and her husband clashed over Brooke; the other children resented the attention Brooke received. Emma had always found succor in looking to the future—Brooke would eventually leave home and become responsible for herself—but as her problems steadily worsened, the future became frightening.

A recurring theme of the stories in this research is the magic of pen and paper. Emma taught herself to release her frustrations and encounter her disappointments by writing down her thoughts. Rather than let her hostilities roam through her mind, raping and pillaging her happier, more useful thoughts, she would capture her negative thoughts on paper to expose them and let them escape. Unlike those individuals who use their writing as reference documents, Emma would simply discard hers, so many Kleenex of the id and ego.

But Emma more and more often encountered her future in her writing—a future irrefutably unsatisfactory. Although she could throw her writing away, she could not rid herself of her anticipated problems, nor of her daughter.

> It got worse, more intense. We had to start counseling for the whole family, which seemed to highlight the conflicts rather than reduce them. I no longer could picture her getting better. All I could picture was the problem getting worse. We began to see the start of a drug problem. We already had a promiscuity problem that was getting worse. I had always thought that "time heals all wounds," but I could not just leave things alone and wait for healing. It would be too late; the family would be destroyed.

Time does heal wounds, but when the new wounds are opened faster than the old ones heal, time is a problem, not a solution. Emma discovered her hopeless future in her writing: Her daughter would be worse; Emma was near collapse; Emma's husband was contemplating leaving; the other children were miserable. Emma had her Realization.

> I had to make some decisions about myself. I couldn't live my daughter's life for her. I decided to stop trying to live her life, trying to involve her, trying to save her. I decided I was tired of misery.

Emma had decided to remove herself emotionally from her daughter, but she still had not decided to quit.

I decided to give up my involvement with Brooke, but not to force her to move—that was a decision I wanted someone else to make.

While the hopelessness of the future had brought Emma to a decision, she had not solved her problem. Emma's efforts to change her perspective without changing her position only heightened her guilt, increasing her emotional burden. Eventually, she checked herself into a hospital, exhausted, broken. There she continued to contemplate her future, continued to write out her thoughts. She finally asserted her Self-interest, deciding to save herself and the rest of the family by finding a new home for Brooke. She recalls her Clean Decision:

> My husband picked me up at the hospital one afternoon, and we went for a drive in the country. We got lost and ended up driving for several hours. My thoughts about Brooke had been in my mind constantly. I knew for weeks, maybe months, what I wanted to do, but I couldn't do it. Finally, we were driving along, not speaking, just driving, and I turned to my husband and said, "Enough already." I'm not sure he even knew at the time what I meant. But it was my decision, and it just bubbled over from all the thinking I had done, and I said it. I had decided.
>
> From then on everything changed. The very next day we started looking for a place for Brooke to live.
>
> I never regretted the decision—just that I had to make a decision. I had admitted that I couldn't help her. It was a matter of survival, my survival, I finally reached the point where I didn't really care what she wanted.

Emma found a family that agreed to take Brooke. They offered the child more freedom and a chance to start anew; Brooke responded well and tried to cooperate. Emma was able to regain her happiness, including a happy family life.

The Case in Perspective

Emma's case exemplifies relationships that seem "unquittable"—where no alternatives seem to exist. Despite attempts to change, the relationship stayed untenable. If Emma had not quit, she believes that her husband would have left her, and her other children would have been permanently affected, leaving her only one dependent, destructive child. By quitting, Emma saved herself, her family, even her daughter Brooke. A sense of a hopeless future caused her Realization (assisted by pencil and paper). After failing in her attempt to quit without quitting (mentally but not physically), Emma asserted her Self-interest and made a Clean Decision.

TAKE THE GUILT AND RUN

If there are indeed the sort of devils imagined by C. S. Lewis in his *Screwtape Letters*—an immense bureaucracy of toadies pursuing selfish goals of advancement by making their human victims unhappy and discontented and thus unworthy of heaven—the lieutenant devil responsible for unhappy marriages obviously takes great pride in his work and in his proudest accomplishment, the mythology that surrounds courtships and weddings. He has constructed an oleaginous, divinely reprehensible system, capable of processing young people into unhappiness with cruel expediency; by the time they realize how ridiculously random the procedure by which they were paired is, they are married, have children, and are too "responsible" to pursue happiness. Heaven (whether on earth or beyond): Denied.

Joannie and Gary were destined to be college sweethearts; he was president of the best fraternity on campus; she, president of the most hotly pursued sorority. Handsome, charming, and headed, it seemed, for Harvard Law School, Gary was one of the few men Joannie would grant the flash of her eyes, smile, skirt. She could be haughty: She was cover-girl pretty and bright, as if her parents—from one of the city's best families—had purchased her genes full-retail at Tiffany's. Both Joannie and Gary realized that the other was the fulfillment of the collegiate dream—the most desirable boy or girl on campus. Gary gave

Joannie a ring; Joannie gave Gary what was left of her virginity (he being her second lover, but the first when she was sober). Neither considered the future; neither gave any thought to their fundamental incompatibility. They both blithely assumed that they would be married shortly after college and would assume the fine life for which they had been bred.

The future first intruded when Joannie's parents insisted on having a wedding date set; the logistics of a nine-hundred-guest wedding required ample reconnaissance and planning. Joannie transferred the pressure to Gary, who responded poorly—he had not heard from Harvard or any other law school, his future was uncertain. Joannie eventually forced Gary to agree to a June date.

Planning the wedding was Gary's first taste of how demanding Joannie could be. He anticipated the pressures he would face in law school, the strain it would put on the marriage, Joannie's selfish response. With his responsibilities in the fraternity, his final-semester course work and the wedding plans, Gary did not dwell on his doubts. He describes overcoming his early hesitation:

> It was never very clear to me why I was reluctant to go ahead with the wedding. Everyone envied me. The one time I confided in my brother, he told me not to be a jerk. Everybody gets cold feet, he told me. I'm not what you would call introspective, so I kinda agreed and forgot about it.

The reassurance worked. (Part of the power of the "cold feet" myth is that it makes the doubt seem as silly, homely, and easily corrected as bare feet. The remaining power comes from the "everybody gets 'em" syndrome; doubt is dismissed as common, even universal, merely the storm before the calm.) Nonetheless, as the wedding date approached, Gary's apprehension intensified.

Then came bad news, four times, and Gary's life was transformed: "I regret to inform you that your application for admission to law school has not been accepted." All four of the top-notch law schools he applied to turned him down. The only acceptance he got was from a low-rated state school. Gary decided, No, it wasn't worth that much. To his list of activities Gary added a job search.

Joannie took the news well at first; she was supportive. Gary's parents only thinly concealed the fact that they were crestfallen. Gary was the son of an overbearing mother, who had lived vicariously through him, driving him to succeed. Gary's father was trying to hold together his auto dealership while his health failed.

> My mother put a lot of pressure on me to stay close to home. She needed me psychologically. I felt I had let her down when I didn't get into law school, and with Dad's health going, I felt awfully sorry for her. Joannie was a different religion, and that bothered Mother, but she was close to Joannie personally. All of that was in my mind, but I can't say that any of that was the reason for my decision not to get married.

Gary spoke of his "decision" not to be married, but it was less a decision than impulsive flight. He felt great uncertainty, grave anxiety, but he refused to voice his concerns to his volatile fiancée. Instead, he began to dwell on nightmarish visions of his future: He foresaw violent clashes with Joannie, ending in a divorce that would break his mother's heart and perhaps literally kill his father.

At least three weeks before the scheduled wedding ceremony, he began to feel that he would not go through with the marriage, but he made no decision. He listened to Joannie's breathless description of the wedding showers and cheerfully opened the wedding gifts that had began to pour into the home of Joannie's parents a few days after nearly a thousand invitations had been mailed. Finally, the night before the rehearsal, two nights before the wedding, Gary and Joannie were alone in her parents' home, having spent the evening opening gifts. He blurted out his doubts. Joannie was apoplectic. As if told of a sudden death of a parent, she refused to believe what she heard; it was simply too incredible for her mind to assimilate. Gary eventually made clear to her that he could not go through with the wedding. She demanded an explanation; he could not provide a convincing one. Sometime after dawn she threw him out of the house. They did not see each other for six months. The shame was so great that Gary went out of the country to spend the remainder of the summer working in the Bahamas; Joannie moved to New York, accepting a job offer she had not even considered until the wedding plans were terminated.

Gary had fled the relationship, but he was not sure why. It had not been hopeless, only uncertain. He had neither a strong Realization nor the conviction of a Clean Decision to ensure against self-doubt and regret. He began to miss Joannie and his chance to have her as his wife. When he happened to "run into her" at a restaurant they had frequented, he and she felt the old spark and eventually began to date again. However, Gary's previous sudden departure caused a considerable distance in the renewed relationship and added to Joannie's parents' total enmity toward Gary; in other words, the relationship was fated. They continue to spend time together, but their relationship is built on memories rather than sympathies.

The Case in Perspective

Gary's quit was destined to fail: Although he fantasized about the future of the relationship, he did not have a clear Realization, never experienced hopelessness, never carefully considered his Self-interest. He was not in a position to make a Clean Decision; had he acted sooner, he might have delayed the wedding until he had resolved his family problems and decided on a career, putting himself in a better position to make a defensible decision. Instead, he avoided his doubts, bolting at the last minute. Gary had not provided himself with any of the emotional insurance against regret; he was an easy target for doubt and self-reproach.

SEARCHING FOR HARMONY

Two simple, similar melodic lines of music can become profound and inspiring when placed in counterpoint. Two of the quitting cases encountered in this research were remarkably parallel—with the critical distinction that one was successful and one was not. Jessica and Spencer, both talented California musicians, faced major career-quitting decisions.

When she was six years old, Jessica's favorite game was hiding while she listened to her older sister practice the piano, then trying to replicate the music by ear and from memory. Only when she was eight did Jessica's parents let her begin piano lessons. Following her skills, Jessica wound up as a music major in college, minoring in education as a sop to the reality of postcollege employment possibilities. Unwilling to accept the rigors of a career as a performer, she accepted a teaching job in a high school in an upper-middle-class white neighborhood. She began the job midyear, after the sudden resignation (after twenty years of service but ten or more years before normal retirement) of the highly regarded music director. Jessica inherited a championship orchestra, undefeated in statewide competitions, but students who were cocky and resentful over the loss of their coach and friend. Like most other young teachers, Jessica was shocked by her undisciplined students, offended by a seemingly indifferent administration. She describes her first months of teaching:

> I was asked to come in for an interview, and a week later I had the job if I could start the following Monday. The whole process took less than two weeks, which seemed fishy. Here it was, just before Festival, when the orchestra would be adjudicated; no conductor would abandon his orchestra just before Festival. His school orchestra gave concerts all over the United States. It made no sense, unless he had terminal cancer or something awful; but there was no explanation to me or to the students, which was a detriment, because he was a father-figure type whom many of the students just worshipped. I was there when he announced to them that he would be leaving: All of a sudden everybody burst into tears, some ran from the room, too shocked to do anything else.
>
> The students were real nice to me for about two weeks; then they started testing me. I didn't get any support

from the administration as far as discipline was concerned. I would send them to the assistant principal and
ask him to discipline them, and they would be back in
class a few minutes later and say, "The assistant principal
said I should be better and not act up and go back to
class." So what could I use as a goad if they had no fear of
the assistant principal? They would steal my roll book,
steal my keys, scrape away the putty from the windows so
that with the next wind that came along, the window
would crash to the ground—everything.

They only pulled together at performances; they were
good, and they were proud. We continued to be the best.
One major drawback to teaching was being handed a
group so good; it would have taken years for me to have
an impact, and a change could only be for the worse.

Jessica began to contemplate quitting teaching during her second month. She shared the unsatisfied teacher's fear: If not
teaching, what? Teaching jobs are difficult to get; an employment file marked "resigned" is believed to be the equivalent of
one marked "Arrested for Felony." Jessica and her peers knew
that there would be no coming home for a quitter and they were
trained for nothing else.

But Jessica encountered her future in the form of a man retiring after forty-two years of teaching. He informed Jessica that
he had detested his last ten or fifteen years. If he could have
started over again, he would never choose teaching. "Use your
talents where they'll be appreciated," was his advice. Another
thought came to Jessica: The students would stay the same, as
would the coursework—no change, no progress, counting the
seasons until retirement.

Teaching is martydom. You have to have a personality
that can adjust to a thankless job. You tolerate all the
problems, all the time, so you can hear, "It was wonderful" twice a year from some tone-deaf parents? It has to
be in your blood. My principal told me that the only
teachers on the faculty who were genuinely happy were
those who could think of no other profession—if they

couldn't be teachers, they would shrivel and die. He told me that unless a teacher could honestly say that of all the jobs in the world they would choose teaching, they would never cut it. He said that, and I was listing about two dozen other jobs I would rather have—none of them, of course, a job for which I was qualified.

Jessica had seen her future and found it unacceptable, but had no other convenient alternative. She vacillated, knowing that she was not born to teach, knowing that she was educated to do nothing else.

Jessica's relationship with her students began to improve when they learned the apparent explanation for the sudden departure of the preceding music director: He had been sexually involved with one of his students, a girl from a broken home. In reaction to this, the students asserted their normalcy by embracing the prim, very conventional Jessica, admitting in effect that they had unconsciously blamed her for the departure of the previous director. For the first time there were good times. The students would stop by after school with their instruments and "jam" with Jessica; for the first time the students invited her to become involved in their lives. Whereas Jessica had been leaning toward quitting, she found herself completely indecisive. She had envisioned her future, had had a Realization (although not a particularly strong one), was able to be self-interested (no one else would be gravely affected by her decision), but she was unable to make a Clean Decision. Eventually, she would have had another, stronger Realization or grown more attached to her work and decided to stay, but she ran out of time; the last day before she had to ask for a renewal of her contract, she quit.

> There just came a deadline when I had to say yes or no. On the day of the deadline I said no. If I had to tell him on the day before I might have said yes. I was weighing it heavily on both sides, and I never really came to a decision.

Without the conviction that arises from a Clean Decision, Jessica was open to regret. She did not have the assurance that comes from knowing exactly why she made her decision, so that when she later questioned it, she had no ready answer.

Well, after I quit, I felt real homesick. I had to turn in my keys and I had to gather up all my plants and all my stuff. I kept saying to myself, "This is the last time I'm going to walk through this door or go to that meeting." From the day I resigned, I dreamed about school every night. And every day since school ended, when I drive past the school, I look over there wistfully and I think, you know, "There was my parking space."

Naturally Jessica recovered from despondency; being a bright and aggressive woman, she rebounded and made a success of a different career. Although she is still occasionally wistful about teaching, she has not attempted to reenter the field. She does admit that she now wishes she had given teaching at least two or three years so that she could have had a fuller experience and made a more trenchant decision.

The Case in Perspective

Jessica had pulled together all the elements of a successful quit except a Clean Decision. Although she had rejected the future she foresaw in teaching, she had not fully explored the profession, had not developed an immediate personal acceptance of its hopelessness as her career. Jessica had relied on her early impressions, the counsel of others, and the pressure of a deadline to make her decision. She did not allow her mind to reach a conclusion, so that her mind did not cease its debate. She needed the additional input that another year of teaching would have provided.

THE JOYFUL MUSIC OF QUITTING

Unlike Jessica's parents, who were reluctant to undertake the expense of piano lessons too soon, Spencer's parents, both with more musical talent than training, urged Spencer to study piano to the point of badgering him. It was the constant pressure of practicing at home that led Spencer to the church organ—that and the big sound, which vented his frustrations. Spencer escaped to a neighborhood church to practice and lose himself in what he calls "wailing." Eventually he became an organ major in college, then studied at a special school for cathedral organists. Upon graduation Spencer was selected (from among over fifty applicants) to fill a full-time position at a new cathedral in the Pacific northwest, as organist and music director. It was an honor rarely conferred on someone so young; Spencer had assumed that he would have to work for many years before having "the ultimate," a cathedral directorship.

The unexpected victory robs the victor of anticipation and preparation; the longer the journey, the sweeter the arrival. To attain "the ultimate" a few months after college cheapens the goal. Already at the top, Spencer had to learn the compromises that were normally a part of reaching the top. He explains his early concessions:

> The first clash came with the first wedding. My training had dictated no secular music, to do away with "Here Comes the Bride" and the other piece, Mendelssohn. but at the cathedral, if the bride had to have it, she was allowed to have it. As a cathedral, we were setting the standards for the diocese in matters of worship. The diocese was an area including millions of people, and here we were allowing this old dead thing just because the bride's mother insisted . . . the bride herself rarely cared. So I played the traditional marches whenever requested and played them magnificently. I had resentment, and I had two tongues in each cheek, but nobody knew the difference.

Spencer's opposition to the traditional wedding marches became only a minor irritation; he soon had a list of objections ranging from the general to the specific.

> A few years after I assumed my position, the cathedral became caught up in the larger liturgical changes taking place, mostly an effort to bring the congregation into greater participation. The level of music had to come down to reach them. In cathedral training, we always pre-

sented music with the ultimate in worship, offering the very best we could. But at the cathedral some of the music we did became sleazy. Now, it's kind of nothing, you know, you go in and half-expect to find a guitar and a drum floating around somewhere and folk-type music— I'm reconciled to that now, but I wasn't then—my background was too rigid. My background gave me no flexibility.

At one of the services, I remember so well, they had an actor come in to give the sermon as Jesus. I had so much trouble with that that I don't even remember playing the next service. I went in the next Monday and said to the dean, "I need to tell you something. I can't serve you in my capacity if you are going to have this kind of garbage. I'm just not able to do it. If you need my resignation, it's here." I felt I had integrity. That kind of thing is a debasement, just a gimmick. If worship can't stand on its own without gimmickery, it doesn't deserve to make it.

Spencer did not resign. The actor episode was a turning point in Spencer's career, for it was the first time he contemplated quitting; it was his Realization.

But Spencer's job was not without its rewards; Spencer describes the profound thrill of knowing he had done it well:

The greatest thrill was not the performance per se so much as when I sensed the congregation was receiving a message. You can tell; for example, during the offering, when the choir is doing something that the congregation is absorbing, you don't hear the money going into the plate. I don't mean that they aren't giving or that they are giving only bills; I'm saying there is a sense of quietness that lets you know they are participating with the choir in an act of worship. That was all that mattered.

The thrill of worship came less frequently than Spencer's discoveries that the cathedral had a different practical Christianity than his own. He saw too many clergymen in hypocritical situations, being philistine as well as divine, acting as donors of advice they could not apply in their own lives. His sense of hypocrisy increased when he began to encounter difficult problems with his personal life. He "screamed out for help" but no one heard. As his dissatisfaction with the cathedral grew, his conviction not to be part of the cathedral's tenth anniversary two years hence waxed also. He felt that ten years at the cathedral would simply be too long; he could only repeat himself, risking his sense of accomplishment. He thus had both a Realization and a sense of the future.

The role as a cathedral organist was no longer the ultimate in Spencer's life. He contemplated alternative futures as his opinion of the cathedral worsened.

> The cathedral was no different from the state government. No different. The politics were too much. From where I stood, I could see through all the cracks, the mechanics instead of the faith. I was not seeing faith, I was seeing what was generating the sparks to give an illusion of faith. The cathedral is a social place. You go there to get married. You make an appearance there if you are a doctor or lawyer who wants to be called prominent.

Spencer's determination to leave the cathedral before becoming redundant and his Realization that the cathedral was not the place of worship he desired were very much on his mind as the annual Christmas pageant was being prepared. It was his eighth year with the cathedral with two years still to go before the tenth anniversary he had vowed he would not witness as an employee. The Christmas Eve program was especially vexing, for it was the most contrived, most mechanical performance of the year—the local NBC-affiliate broadcast the midnight service each year.

> I believe that the dean of the cathedral was a frustrated actor. He would be a very fine one, it was his element. The TV show was the highlight of his year, and he wanted everything to be resoundingly perfect. The pageantry and the vestments were exciting, but everything was so carefully worked out that you feared even one miscue; they would critique the playback very carefully. Personally, I didn't want to be reminded, because I always

goofed up, or some chorister would faint or throw up in the hallway.

We were catering to the television audience, and, literally, the hell with the guy in the pew.

During the Christmas service I decided to quit. That night everything was lifted from my shoulders. If there is such a thing as the Holy Spirit, I felt it, just then and there. No regrets. It was my first decision to do something on my own. So when it came down to Christmas Eve, I had, as far as I was concerned, fulfilled my obligations to everybody else, and it was now time for my obligations to myself.

Spencer resigned the following week. He found a teaching position and a job as a part-time accompanist to a choir. No regrets.

The Case in Perspective

Like Jessica, Spencer had a number of Realizations. Neither Jessica nor Spencer was overly conscious of alternative futures (unlike other successful quitters). Neither was impaired by unselfish considerations. Unlike Jessica, the music teacher, Spencer did not rush his decision; in fact, he decided to quit almost two years before his self-imposed deadline for leaving.

By allowing himself time for a Clean Decision, Spencer had left far less ground where guilt or remorse could sprout and flourish.

THE ENDLESS DECISION

Teen-agers used to pay four dollars to hear her sing for an evening; now businessmen pay fifty dollars to be abused by her for an hour. This is not progress. Ming, a lithe Oriental beauty, was for three years the lead singer for a rock band. She insists that she is still a singer, but Ming has not sung before an audience for nearly two years. (Calculating just how long it had been perplexed, then surprised Ming; she had airily dismissed her time off as "about a year." Asked for specific dates, the fact that it was really two years seemed to startle her.) Ming has quit singing, but not only did she not make a decision to quit, she is reluctant to admit that she has quit. A part of her reluctance is her refusal to identify with her new career as a hooker specializing in B&D (bondage and discipline); she would prefer to think of her new career as temporary, a pause in her more acceptable career as a musician. She actively regrets quitting her singing career but has not been sufficiently candid with herself to identify what she must do to return to and succeed in singing.

Ming talked about her rock career:

> It wasn't a bad life. I miss it. When it was happening to me, I didn't appreciate it. We were on the road all the time, doing the biggest bars in the smaller towns and the small bars in the big cities. It had its good and bad points, but the band was solid, and we earned some respect. We were working too hard. The leader of the group was in his late thirties; his voice was going—too many years of hard rock, hard life. He knew it was about gone and that he had wasted away his best years, and he tried to make up for it. He would rather be castrated than give up singing—he just wasn't the power on the guitar to go with only that—his voice was his life. So he's in a big hurry to do everything as fast as possible, and then it's still too slow. We were always pushing, always tired. He was rushing to succeed while his voice was still interesting; I no way wanted to use mine up. We fought over that. But he was the boss—we used to call him "the wagonmaster."
>
> At first none of us gave any thought to the future. It looked bad for "the wagonmaster," and none of the rest of us much cared about anything but the next joint and the next sleep. I had a thing going with one of the guys in the band, but we were tired so often that it didn't amount to much. After a good show and a good audience, if we were in some dink town where we didn't have any connections to any action, I would seduce the whole band—all four guys. I'd start singing to them and do a slow dance until they all needed me. I used to have a little line I'd use to let them know I was ready; I'd say, "Let me have your

microphones," and then I'd take turns holding and singing to their crotches until they would just go wild. What I'm saying is, there were some good times, and a girl could live out her fantasies. But there was no future.

Despite Ming's unique performances on and off stage, the band began to lose its cohesion to exhaustion and discontent. The crowds varied, but they were large and receptive more often than they were disappointing. Nonetheless, the sensation of arousing a crowd diminished from a jolt to a jingle. The band grew jaded, needed a new challenge. The aging leader could only do more of the same; he was unable to accept the experimentation that might have enabled the group to distinguish itself. Instead, through internal bickering, the group extinguished itself. Two of the five members left, pleading with Ming to join them. She remained loyal, although she is not certain why. The quick replacements for the departed pair were inadequate; the group lost its magic. Ming could still ignite a crowd, but she had grown haggard and rarely tried. When the group spent a night in New York City before driving to Boston to help open a club, Ming slipped away. No good-byes. She just left.

I was very, very tired. I had been arguing with Hal, the group's leader, and I just wanted to get away. We weren't going anywhere and we never would. I had friends in New York, so I went to them. I didn't want to tell the guys I was leaving and cause some big-deal reaction.

When she left, Ming told herself that she would find a new group and be back on stage within a few weeks; first, she would take a vacation. One price of having literally slipped into the darkness was the requirement of traveling light. She had taken only an overnight bag and sixty-three dollars. In order to have time to rest and money to acquire a new wardrobe, Ming needed a part-time job, but not singing, she told herself; she had earned a vacation. A friend of a friend told her where she could earn several hundred dollars a week in a legal sex parlor. Ming describes the job:

It's a large apartment in a not-bad neighborhood in Manhattan. Guys come in who are into bondage or pain. I tie them up, maybe beat them up a little—whatever their fantasy is. Some want a good spanking, some want a pin stuck through their foreskin. I assist in the fantasy. I'm more of an actress than a hooker, because I never have sex with them. They get themselves off. I'm just kind of a human *Playboy* foldout that fulfills their particular fantasy.

The pay is good, and the hours are convenient; Ming considers it a desirable job. But it isn't singing. And Ming still says she's a singer. She hasn't done serious voice exercises in three years. She hasn't performed in over two. She has few active contacts. She has no plans to change.

I'm making some progress at the place I work. It's helping me get my head around. Just the other day there was a man, a big black man who wanted to be whipped with a bullwhip he brought. Before, I would turn that over to one of the tougher girls, but I did this one myself. I did pretty good, too. I gave it to him. I pulled it off—he's already been back and asked to see me.

Ming has developed a clientele and, like any retailer, is reluctant to abandon her good and profitable customers. Her singing career was never hopeless, and she never intended to abandon it; by refusing to admit that she has quit, she maintains some of the glamour and glory of her previous career, but she keeps her prostitution from becoming admittedly hopeless, a prerequisite for quitting. Thus, barring some miracle—say, a man who, between tortures, mentions that he is a rock impresario looking for a female singer—Ming has none of the typical catalysts to quitting. Only when she admits that her future is taking her further into B&D and farther away from singing will she be forced to realize the hopelessness of her current career and to take action to change.

The Case in Perspective

This case was chosen to exemplify one end of the Clean Decision continuum. While Ming had some glimpses of the hopelessness of her future with her particular group, she did not accept the hopelessness of her singing career. Thus, she was not headed for a successful quit. Impulsively, she quit anyway. She ran and hid. There were no elements of a Clean Decision. She did not have a commitment to quitting at even a conscious level. She did not decide to leave her career; she is standing by while her career leaves her. She misses singing and wishes she had followed through on the leads she had just after leaving the group. She is so inert that she will probably not admit to herself that she has quit singing until it is safely too late to undertake the rigors of training, practice, and performance anew. She has left herself woefully open to remorse, bitterness, and a sense of failure.

BILL RUSSELL

Major life decisions are often marked by physical manifestations that arise at the climax of a difficult mental process. Bill Russell, in his memoirs *Second Wind*, describes two decisions that were such mental cataclysms that he *felt* them instead of just making them. The first of these two decisions occurred when Russell was just a junior in high school, faced with all the usual adolescent adjustments and uncertainties, plus those that come from being black and freakishly tall. Russell had his life changed while walking the length of a school corridor. The walk was alone and uninterrupted, save by this thought, "Hey, you're all right." To Russell it was a "mystical revelation." His whole life changed. The Realization was so vivid that it "seemed to have colors," and Russell spent the rest of the day giving circumspect looks to his classmates "to make sure the other kids didn't think I was acting strange." Suddenly he was certain that he was O.K.; it was, according to Russell, a "religious experience." Whether religious or not, a warm feeling enveloped his body, and he felt and acted differently.

Another "felt" quitting decision came during his struggle to decide when to retire from professional basketball. It was his thirteenth season and was to be the eleventh Celtic championship year. Russell was by then the Celtics player-coach, and this gave him fewer chances to lose himself in playing. He had to see more than his own role, had to decide team strategy. In addition, he was getting older, not better. Some of the quickness was gone, some of the moves were just not there when he reached for them. Russell had told himself that there are "no final victories in sports"; the games are larger than the men who play them. Russell played several seasons knowing he had passed the zenith of his physical talent, and could have played several more, but in the 1968–69 season he began to lose the joy of the game when it "dawned" on him that he could no longer ignite his team. He told himself that it would be his last season; he had had his Realization, admitted his future, and asserted his Self-interest. His Clean Decision was to be next.

Midway through the season the Celtics played the Bullets in Baltimore. The Celtics came from behind late in the game to tie the score, then stole the ball in the final seconds to have one last chance to win. With the crowd screaming in excitement and the exhilarated players hopping about in anticipation, the Celtics called time out and huddled close to Russell, their coach, who was leading the cheers, yelling, "Now we've got 'em! Let's go out there and kill 'em!" But as his team watched in amusement that quickly turned to dismay, Russell burst into laughter— uncontrollable laughter. His team asked for the last-shot play. Russell just laughed. He described what happened:

> I was wiping my eyes, recovering from hysterics, and shaking my head because a thought had just lit on my shoulder out of nowhere. I said, "Hey, this is really something. Here I am a grown man, thirty-five years old, running around semi-nude in front of thousands of people in Baltimore, playing a game and yelling about killing people. How's that?" I looked at my teammates as if I'd really said something profound, and they looked back blankly as if I hadn't said anything.

The denouement of the story is that Russell's Celtics threw the ball away and lost. The end of the more important story is that Russell made his Clean Decision during the game. He thought he had already decided to retire, but the fit of laughter removed all doubt, for it demonstrated the psychological distance between him and his sport. Over several seasons of agonizing about retirement, he had been subconsciously removing himself from the game, until finally, during the Bullets game, he could see himself as an outsider would (a complete outsider, not even a fan), and he mocked himself. All levels of his mind were ready for retirement.

Bill Russell in Perspective

A clean quitting decision often results from objectifying the quitting situation. Suddenly the unsatisfactory relationship is externalized, literally seen as if by a new person. Hope for improvement can then become laughable; unselfishness can become ridiculous. The decision is abruptly as simple as the advice friends outside the relationship give: "Just go." Bill Russell knew that he had made his decision when he began to see his sport as silly. Having passed through a Realization and the other components of successful quitting, he knew what his decision had to be; his Clean Decision was a fiat to himself, removing all doubt and hesitation.

THE RELATION OF THE CLEAN DECISION TO SUCCESSFUL QUITTING

The Clean Decision is the moment when the mind says, "That's it. Case Closed." Here is how that happened in each of the examples of this chapter.

- Although she waited eight and a half years to implement her decision, Mary, the woman with the goal of a big-city and government job, never wavered in her decision to leave the man who tied her down to small-town ennui. The Clean Decision removed doubt, allowing Mary to devote her mental energies to the difficult issue of getting out of her marriage.

- Emma faced an "unquittable" situation—a daughter who was tearing her family apart. Yet, after years of agonizing, she was able to make a Clean Decision and accomplish the unthinkable.

- Gary left his fiancée on the eve of their wedding. Because he postponed a decision so long, he had no time for sublimation, no time for the other components of successful quitting to give his decision a strong framework. Without a Clean Decision, Gary was open to guilt and regret.

- Jessica psychologically committed herself to giving up her teaching career before she could deeply explore the implications of quitting. Had her decision been made a day earlier or a day later, she might have remained in teaching and might have been happier. Because she recognized the uncertainty of her decision when it was made, she constantly replays it in her mind, often reaching a different conclusion. Regret is not knowing why a decision was made.

- Spencer, the organist, reached into his subconscious for his quitting decision (or maybe it reached into him). On Christmas Eve, during what should have been his proudest moment, he delivered himself into a new life.

- Ming not only failed to make a Clean Decision, she failed to acknowledge that she had really made a decision at all—a decision to retire from her singing career. Hers was the most imperfect of decisions—barely conscious—and destined to be unsuccessful.

- Bill Russell lifted himself out of professional basketball when he rose beyond his sport to see his rump-slapping, ball-bouncing self as ridiculous. He accepted this message from himself and made a Clean Decision to retire.

THE RULE

Once the Futuring, the Realization, and the assertion of Self-interest have taken an individual through the door of a decision to leave, the Clean Decision closes and locks the door. Such quitters are united within themselves and are irrevocably committed to act. The Clean Decision is thus the fourth of the four key components to successful quitting.

EXCEPTIONS TO THE RULE

Events may toss an individual from a relationship before a Clean Decision can be made. If the relationship was so oppressive that the quitter immediately gains a better life, the quit is immediately rewarded; there is no appearance of guilt, and the quit is likely to be successful. In such a circumstance no decision is made: It is the fact of having left, rather than the decision to leave, that is affirmed. This is a Clean Decision after the fact: The results of the quit make it clear that the decision to leave was (or would have been) correct, whether or not it was actually made.

Other cases were encountered where individuals claimed to have successfully quit a relationship without reaching a Clean Decision and without being pushed from the relationship. Roberto was one of these cases. Having come from a family of first-generation wealth, his parents regarded ambition and its rewards as commandments. Roberto simply did not possess either the personality or the intellect to attain worldly success. He failed in four careers, one engagement to be married and one marriage. Driven from within and without, Roberto became a shrugger. His shoulders round, his walk a shuffle, he was perpetually ready to admit defeat and, with a shrug, to move on. Growing tired of a failing relationship, Roberto would just walk away. No Clean Decision. Yet of the five quitting decisions Roberto would recall in detail, four appeared to be successful. In Roberto's case, the apparent success of the quits came as a result of a larger, but no cleaner, decision. In effect, Roberto had realized that by his parents' standards, which had become his own, he was hopeless. When he enters a relationship, he has already failed, already admitted it is hopeless.

Roberto already made his decision to quit trying to succeed a long time ago. This enables him to quit a given career or personal relationship without additional remorse. The larger decision, the one to give up on succeeding, is the one decision he

truly regrets. He spoke of the pain and loneliness of a proud
failure:

> The only job I've ever had that I really enjoyed was work-
> ing in the warehouse of Montgomery Ward putting to-
> gether bicycles and other equipment for the Christmas
> rush. The man who hired me kept trying to get me to take
> a different job with Montgomery Ward's. I told him I
> liked my job. He told me that they liked me and that the
> job I had would end right after Christmas and they would
> have to let me go. Since I had a lot of education and stuff,
> they wanted me to work inside, in sales. Finally they per-
> suaded me to sell men's suits. I hated it. Mostly I was
> afraid I would see someone I knew. All my relatives and
> the kids I grew up with are doctors and lawyers, and I
> didn't want to be seen there. I also didn't want to have to
> talk to people by force. I like people, but not to have to
> talk to them. The second day I just walked out at lunch
> and never came back. I never picked up my check, al-
> though it wasn't much, of course.

Roberto never regretted leaving Ward's; clearly he did regret
leaving his family and friends rather than allow the possibility of
public failure. Because he did not recognize his broader
decision—to leave his family and friends—he was not able to
confront his mistake directly. He continues to quit insignificant
careers without remorse, for these quits are merely the mean-
derings of a lost person. Without a destination there are no
wrong turns.

The Clean Decision in Perspective

The moment of the Clean Decision is when an individual can
say, "You are not what you quit." This is not the moment of
physical departure; it is the moment of mental objectification or
externalization, when the person knows he will quit and almost
coolly begins to plot the implementation of the decision. The
Clean Decision occurs when the subconscious and conscious
levels of the mind unite in a decision. Because these two parts of
the mind operate at different speeds, responding differently to

various events, months or years may pass before they join for a quitting decision. However, the other three elements of successful quitting seem to funnel the mind toward a Clean Decision. The Futuring, Realization, and Self-interest variables focus the decision, leading a potential quitter to the brink; the Clean Decision is the fateful last step. Should the individual hesitate too long at the edge of a decision, another view of the future or an additional Realization may give the reluctant person the final shove.

PATHS DOWN THE

MOUNTAIN

. . . a great step. Yes, in seriousness, a very great step, for which all the walking in his life had not prepared him. Not an easy step, nor an easy journey, it would take an eternity as the anvil ever fell. His strained bowels sagged; his hurt leg cursed; his head felt light. The whiteness of limestone pierced his eyes. A little breeze met his face at the cliff-edge. His will, a perfect diamond under the pressure of absolute fear, uttered the final word. Now.

John Updike
The Centaur

THE "perfect diamond" of will formed by the pressure of fear is the Clean Decision. The Clean Decision is the will to act; determination is the shadow that pulls the body. The will matters more than the manner, the decision more than the device. The nature of the journey to the cliff-edge of quitting is significant; the will to go one more step is significant; the height of the plunge is not. Majestic or craven, sudden or lingering, proud or fearful: The great step is a great step.

The speed or manner of implementing the quitting decision is not related to successful quitting; *if* a person quits is what matters, not the nature of the departure. This was the wisdom of the Gravel Plan to end the Vietnam War: During the war Senator

Gravel was asked how he would get American troops out of Vietnam. He replied, "Some by air, some by boat." The Gravel Plan recognized that that great societal failure to quit, the Vietnam War, should simply be ended. Having admitted to failure, the relevant concern was the curtain, not the final scene.

The paradoxes of inaction and the philosophical prejudice against acknowledging how important individual circumstances are to happiness has created "exit phobia." Even when the combined momentum of Futuring, Realization, and Self-interest propel a person to a resolve to quit, the act of quitting remains intimidating; the anticipation is far worse than the reality. Individuals planning to quit vastly overrate the impact of their quitting announcement, expecting but rarely encountering the worst. (Employees who forecast bankruptcy for the departed company were consistently surprised when doom was in reality a ripple, and those who predicted suicide attempts for the marriage partner left behind were annoyed or amused to find the estranged spouse dating or travelling or otherwise delighting in new-found freedom.) Exit phobia is like the common fear of snakes—the terror is out of proportion to the danger. Yet because the dangers of quitting are as real as snake venom, the implementation deserves analysis. In the long run, the nature of the implementation does not affect success; in the short run, pain and dislocation can be minimized.

Before examining several cases that demonstrate the disparity between a strategy of implementation and success, let's look at some of the methods of quitting encountered in this research.

QUITTING STRATEGIES

Three basic strategies for implementing the quitting decision emerged from the cases that were studied: the Clean Break, the Soft Landing, and the Crash Landing. Within these major categories there are variations:

Clean Break: The Precipitous Conclusion

Act, then inform
Present papers (a resignation letter or divorce papers):

A woman who found her husband's month-long absence to play a tennis circuit "the last straw" met her returning spouse at the door, stuck a pen in the hand that reached out to embrace her, then led him to the kitchen table, where his homecoming dinner sat beside divorce papers.

Flee:
One employee took his vacation and never returned. A woman determined to end her engagement simply moved to a new city.

The unmistakable gesture (the dramatic act to announce, more or less directly, the end)·
An obscene phone call to the boss; having a moving company simply appear at the house.

Inform, then act (the classic cards-on-the-table, lay-it-out, own-up confrontation; still popular, this strategy is most often a follow-up to one of the Soft Landing strategies)

Soft Landing: Preparation for the End

Preparation of oneself (a broad category that includes all the readying of oneself, on emotional and material levels, that is necessary for a new life. Often this involves psychological distancing or other ways of hardening one's emotions):
Often some form of experimenting or practicing was engaged in. One man would stare at his sleeping wife and tell himself he hated her. An unsuccessful businessman began taking karate and weight-lifting classes to prepare himself for a new career as a fireman. An unhappily married man started to practice flirting with other women again; another asked an old girl friend to help him brush up on his sexual technique (a favor that she declined, incidentally). Others joined the YMCA, started or stopped attending church, moved to a smaller house, or otherwise changed their life-style.

Preparation of others (fearing that an estranged company

or spouse will not adapt well, the quitter-to-be attempts to prepare them):

Planning to begin a different career, a business consultant hired and trained his replacement for nearly a year. One man was able to convince his wife to get a job, all the while waiting to announce his divorce plans. One woman tried to convince her husband to have an affair in order to reduce the guilt she was feeling about secretly plotting a divorce. Often the preparation is less direct, consisting of cryptic lectures on inner strength or leaving a magazine lying open to an article on starting a new life.

Preparation of both partners (a combination of planning and preparing for both parties to the quit):

Frequently the joint preparations were material—the purchase of a second automobile, saving money, moving. Another common preparation was counseling. Several of those interviewed reported having asked a marriage counselor to end their marriage expeditiously. Taking an overly long vacation was used toward ending both careers and marriages.

Crash Landing. Destroying the Relationship to Walk Away from the Wreckage.

Downward spiral (an attempt to provoke the partner to welcome continually widening emotional distance; similar to the Soft Landing strategy, though it is not a preparation for the end—rather it is intended to *be* the end):

Taking a separate apartment was used as the means to wind down a marriage. Increasingly abusing a company's work system was used, unconsciously, to force a decision to pursue a new career.

"Stick and move" (a phrase used in boxing that means throwing punches while making oneself a moving target; a strategy that comes easily to many who wish to fail; attack, then disappear; the bringing of guerilla tactics to

personal relationships; a familiar strategy that eventually
drains the will of the partner *qua* opponent):
> Verbal conflict between the people in a relationship is
> banal, shamelessly familiar. More interesting and more
> shameless were the attempts to booby-trap a relation-
> ship physically: One woman had made a list of an-
> noyances she could use, including burning her hus-
> band's toast, scraping crumbs into his jelly, losing his
> socks, and writing checks she knew would bounce.

Half crash (a half quit, such as a separation or a leave of
absence; usually the first bounce after leaping off the
cliff; when combined with a downward spiral or a "stick
and move," it permits the relationship's losses to be taken
by physical separation of the parties):
> Temporarily taking a job in another city was one
> method used to force a quit. Another was an extended
> visit to ill relatives.

War (the use of all the emotional or physical weapons that
the minds of human beings can conceive):
> A man put a pair of his mistress's pantyhose in his glove
> compartment, then asked his wife to get him the map
> he kept there. An unsuccessful poet burned his poems
> to convince himself to abandon his art.

Given a determination to quit, the conventional wisdom dic-
tates a Clean Break as the most honorable, reliable, and effective
means of dissolving the bond. Yet, as we have seen, the cleanness
of the implementation was not related to success. Further, the
Clean Break rarely produced the classic dignified exit. The
Clean Break is often *too* sudden; the actions of the startled parties are unpredictable. Some who felt that a Clean Break was the
honorable solution discovered that the honorable deed was inter-
preted (perhaps correctly) as "insensitive." Because the Clean
Break was often seen as sudden, suspicions and other defenses
were raised to an unnaturally high level. Individuals who, without warning, asked for a divorce were often accused of "having
found someone else." The person who abruptly resigns is also

viewed with suspicion. "I wonder what his *real* reasons are," was a typical reaction.

By waiting for the relationship to crash-land, the *moment* of departure was easier on those who were being left; it was even welcome. No suspicions were raised, and fewer obstacles of any kind were constructed by the weary partners. But being a pilot who is determined to crash-land has its price, its dangers. It not only takes time (months, even years), but it is time spent in the nastiest sort of way—prompting arguments, causing failure. Moreover, the physical danger of a violent reaction is quite real (as some of the preceding cases have demonstrated). The pilot bent on destruction abjures his right to declare the relationship ended, substituting the lowest form of manipulative behavior to attain his goal.

The most effective, caring approach to quitting lies between the extremes of the Clean Break and the Crash Landing. Several weeks or a few months devoted to greasing the exit were useful, particularly when both sides got the benefit of such preparation. The greater the care taken by the one who quits to minimize disruption in the lives of those being left, the easier the exit—a statement not quite as self-evident as it first appears. People were successful in minimizing disruption principally by material considerations (for example, planning to continue the work flow or acquiring another car) rather than by manipulating emotional states. Plans to bolster the spirits of those being left by appealing for help from friends or arranging activities created resentment more often than they provided succor.

ENDURANCE QUITTING

In the chapter on Futuring we had the inspiring story of Sylvia, the woman who overcame her dependence on an unworthy husband and her poverty by devising a five-year plan for her life and a balance sheet for her quitting decision. Her triumph came not simply in quitting her dismal circumstances, but in her resolve not to be lured back to her former dependence. Sylvia returns in this chapter, for the remainder of her story is an education in acting on a difficult decision.

Recall that Sylvia's husband made a practice of disappearing: a man determined not to collect his winnings, not to allow success in his life. Sylvia eventually gathered the courage to tell him that she wanted a divorce. She took a job and made the necessary arrangements, carefully planning the material aspects of her departure (a new apartment on the bus line so that she could sell the car, and so forth). Before she made any of these overt gestures, she explained her feelings to her husband. When she made no immediate move to leave him, he dismissed her resolve to quit as a mere threat and soon vanished once again. Sylvia moved.

Recognizing the inevitability of her husband's being able to find the family, Sylvia did not hide; rather she prepared. (Sylvia claims that she would have moved to a different state and attempted to hide if only she could have afforded to.) Although she had made her decision to quit alone, unassisted, she sought a family counselor to help with the implementation: Not only did Sylvia want the reassurance of professional advice, she wanted someone whom she would not want to let down and who would therefore help her to keep her courage up; someone to assist the children in their adjustment; and someone who could be a source of help for her husband, should he consent to being helped.

Surprise was Sylvia's great ally when her husband did return: All the changes and her obvious certainty of purpose stunned him. Silenced by the family's new life without him, he asked only for a "small favor," the right to spend a few nights while he found somewhere to stay. Seeking to placate him, Sylvia agreed—but only after having pinned him down, not only to a departure date (four days later) but to a check-out time (noon). Despite his protests, he left on the stated date by the stated time. Sylvia called her ex-husband a "master manipulator": Apparently he guessed that an angry confrontation was just what Sylvia was most prepared for, most insulated against. Instead of a battle, he found an apartment and sweetly offered to help Sylvia with her bills. She took the money but recognized that it was temporary; she knew that once her husband saw he could not buy her continued dependence, the money would stop. Within three weeks her husband had attempted to tie his financial assistance to favors—a visit, a dinner, sex. Sylvia refused to bargain. She reread her balance sheet, recalling the unhappiness of her former life. Thwarted in an attempted rapprochement with Sylvia, her husband turned to trying to charm the children. Soon they were pleading with Mom to let Dad come home. Sylvia withstood even this. Frustrated and angry, he made one final attempt to rejoin his family: In a tense scene, Sylvia told him he would have to kill her if he wanted to move in. Finally persuaded, or perhaps just weary, or perhaps still plotting, he took a new job in a bordering state.

Sylvia had survived. Her victory brought her freedom from fear but not freedom from want; the endless burden of supporting four children on the salary from her unskilled labor was oppressive. Her older children were adolescents and played the eternal game of freeing themselves, testing their environment. Sylvia endured. Her life was hard, but it was hers.

The next test of Sylvia's determination came when she filed for divorce. Her son, seventeen and independent, was angry at his mother and went to live with his father, becoming a sort of volunteer hostage who demanded the reunion of the family. Sylvia described her predicament:

> I had filed for divorce, but my son had taken sides with my husband, which caused me to stop and think. I couldn't help but wonder if I shouldn't have stuck it out a few years longer for the sake of the kids. My husband started calling me once our son had arrived up there. He wanted another chance. He had my son get on the phone and tell me that his father had changed and was now reliable and hardworking.
>
> It got harder, not easier, to say no. At first it was easy because I was angry and like, "Look you, this is what you caused. This is what you deserve." But you get to a point when you aren't angry anymore and you really, honestly feel sorry for him. It isn't easy then.

Despite the continuous pressure of financial distress and emotional battering, Sylvia continued in her resolve. The phone calls from her husband and son came less often; when they came, they brought a sorry message of illness. The father was sick, the son working odd jobs to pay the bills. The son confided that he was thinking about returning. She told him that it had only been four months, he could not "run back and forth," but if, after a total of six months with his father, he wanted to return, he had her permission.

> Six months to the day after my son left home I got a call in the middle of the night—he was at the Greyhound station. He had spent his last money to buy a ticket home. I still didn't have a car, so I told him how to get a bus home. That's when he said to me—and I still haven't forgiven him—"I brought Dad with me." He went on to tell me how sick his father was and how between them they had only ten or twelve dollars and nowhere to go but home. What could I say? I said, "All right." I should have said to my son, "You come home and leave your father to sleep in the bus station," but I didn't.

By the time the prodigal father and son arrived, Sylvia had her speech prepared. She refused the embraces of either father or son until she had stated her demands: Christmas was one week away; the father could stay until the day after Christmas, the son would have to find a job by the first of the year and contribute to the family's support. Both agreed.

Later that night Sylvia's husband told her that he had cancer and was dying. He pleaded with her to let him spend his remaining weeks with his family. Sylvia, skeptical, said only that she would consider his request.

> I checked out his story by calling this doctor he said he had. There is no such doctor. When I confronted him he said he knew it was cancer and didn't want to waste his money on a doctor. This was the one taste of being with him that I needed. I told him I never wanted to see him again. I let him stay there through Christmas, which was ruined by his being there, but then shoved him out the door.

He still comes around occasionally. He's so pathetic that I can't be cruel to him, but I tell him firmly that he can never come back.

The Case in Perspective

While Sylvia's implementation was far from a Clean Break quit, it was a highly successful quit—an example of how implementation need not be related to success. Her implementation involved a great deal of easing the way, which was of assistance in getting the husband to agree to the first separation and permitting her the necessary early resolve; however, she was faced with his continual reappearances. A cleaner break would have eliminated his continuing attempts at reconciliation, but it also—and this was Sylvia's belief—could have set off a violent reaction. Unfortunately, Sylvia's preparation for the end was only for her own survival; there was no way in which she could have provided for her husband's adjustment. Had there been a way to prepare him as well as she was prepared, the end would have been far easier. But the important ending to Sylvia's story is that she was able to find independence and eventually break free of poverty—a happy ending despite the painful breakup of her marriage. It was an unfortunate marriage that could not have had a good end. The happy ending for Sylvia is not *how* she left, but *that* she left.

NO CHANCE

Opposites attract. That was the cliché Suzanne always used when perplexed friends asked her why she chose the husband she did. She—ambitious, cerebral, lively; he—quiet, simple, introverted but not introspective. Perhaps all that brought them together was that she was admired, he was admiring.

These opposites did not merely attract, they banged together and stuck. Suzanne was soon bored by her opposite, then annoyed, then ready to criticize him. She described the latter days of the marriage:

> He told me how much he wanted to share his life with me. Well, his life turned out to be mainly watching television.

Two individuals watching the same ridiculous show was staring, not sharing. I wanted to experience; he wanted to watch. I began to feel like he was my kid brother tagging along everywhere. I had standards; he had a bad back and tired easily. I had to maintain the house, make most of the money, and find my way despite him.

The marriage slowly eroded until I would just avoid him. It got to where I would stay up late reading every night so that he would be asleep by the time I got to bed. Our sex life ended. I would cringe when he touched me.

I started to see things that had never bothered me before: his laugh, for example. On the rare occasions when he laughed in my presence, I would groan inside because his laugh was so absurd.

Suzanne had her Realization when her husband told her that three months had passed since they had made love. "How long do I have to wait?" he asked. She thought long on the question and decided that he would have to wait forever. She saw their future—the slow, painful end of their marriage. Having come to the point of caring little about her husband, she asserted her Self-interest and soon made a Clean Decision. Suzanne immediately began playing practice games to prepare for life after marriage. She adopted the title Ms. rather than Mrs., began flirting, would spend evenings with friends, and often "forgot" to wear her wedding ring. Meanwhile, she silently deliberated the best procedure for ending her marriage. Her nature and her ethics demanded a Clean Break—an honorable, forthright presentation of facts and feelings—however, she could not envision a scenario for a Clean Break that would not leave her friends, relatives, and husband aghast, for none of them suspected what she was planning to do. She knew they would all expect a scenario of second chances and public suffering, which would be a proper notification of the impending end, and she would feel obliged to provide it. She tempered her eagerness for an end to the marriage with the anticipated demand for caution and, moving gradually, settled upon a two-stage withdrawal: She would demand of her husband a clean finish to their marriage, but she would give in to his pleas for another chance and would compromise on a legal separation, to begin with the next disagreement. The separation would serve as the required notification of the impending end, would satisfy their family and friends, and would permit both sides to prepare for the probable divorce.

When the inevitable next disagreement arrived, Suzanne walked.

> I went back home, which was nice. It was a relief to be away from my own house. I stayed at home for six weeks. My husband kept calling, asking when I would be home. I just kept saying, "No, it isn't time yet." I was getting a lot of pressure to give him a second chance, and when he promised me that if I came home and wasn't happy, I could have a divorce without a fight, I agreed to move back in.
>
> I said to myself, "Well, I guess things will be different for two, maybe three days, then it'll be back to the same old problems." Yet I knew that if I moved in for a few weeks, I could end it more easily. My motives were not really to try to start over—I knew too much for that, he'd never be what I needed—but to come to a civil finish.

Naturally, given her attitude, Suzanne's prediction came true: A couple of days of fun, then the old problems were back to stay.

> I had dated some while we were separated, and he found out about it, so he didn't trust me. The second night I was back, I had to go to a baby shower, and he stole my keys and insisted that he drive me there and pick me up. He wanted to guard me. When I came home that night—I got a ride with a friend instead—he wanted to have sex. He started making advances. I didn't want to and I told him I wanted our relationship to be right before I made love to him, because I didn't want my body to be used or lovemaking to be used. This time he was extremely insistent, which turned me off even more. Finally I told him I would sleep in the guest room so that he wouldn't have the agitation of having me in the same bed. He told me that if I slept in the next room, I was a boarder, not a wife,

and I would have to pay for the room. I took a ten-dollar bill out of my purse, slapped it on the chest of drawers, and went and slept in the other room. The next morning I called a mover and I was out within the week.

The final week was emotional: a number of bitter arguments, a brief wrestling session; her husband had the locks changed and got a new, unlisted phone number. Suzanne continued to pursue her plan to move, although as a last concession to her husband she agreed to visit a marriage counselor. She informed the counselor that she would be moving in two days and would not return.

The Case in Perspective

Suzanne's implementation of her quit is a hybrid, somewhere between a Clean Break and a Crash Landing. Her Futuring and Realization enabled her to foresee the hopelessness of enduring the marriage; her Self-interest and Clean Decision enabled her to act resolutely to end the relationship without waiting for the normal process of disintegration. She chose instead to endure as a matter of form an eight-week-long version of the disintegration of her marriage.

In Suzanne's case, this hybrid strategy of implementation worked well. She was able to get a divorce fairly readily, she won the sympathies of friends and relatives by allowing them sufficient time to adjust to the reality of her failed relationship, and both Suzanne and her husband are happy and healthy, even enjoying an occasional lunch together. However, while the implementation worked, it was not related to the success of Suzanne's decision to quit. The key components of success, culminating in a Clean Decision, had ensured that she was following a correct course; the implementation can only be judged on its merits as a short-run means to a predetermined end, and its success evaluated in those terms.

THE TICKING EDUCATIONAL BOMB

If all the suppressed and repressed hostility of America's teachers should be released the explosion would level this country's educational system. The aphorism "Those who can, do. Those who can't teach" would be modified by resentful teachers to read, "Those who can, quit. Those who can't, are due—due more money, more respect, more administrative cooperation." A surplus of teachers' labor and a self-selection process that brings mainly traditional values into the profession has put a heavy lid on the vexations and alienation of the modern school teacher. The teacher's specialized skill makes it difficult to move readily into other occupations. The pressure under the lid grows.

Ginger was once part of America's least-appreciated profession. She described herself as a teacher "ready to explode":

> The wave of human-rights assertiveness that rolled over us in reaction to Vietnam and the civil rights movement crushed the system of discipline in our schools. Learning *is* discipline. Discipline teaches children discipline and teaches them how to learn. The broadcast media go around in their hair shirts blaming themselves for the decline in college admission test scores. What vanity! It is simply lack of discipline that has caused the decline. Discipline.
>
> I began as an elementary school teacher with a part-time job at night in a local junior college. In the junior-college classes the students tended to fall into the category of that other aftereffect of Vietnam, the GI Bill student. They mostly slept through class. It was a job to them—a job that paid fairly well, from which they could not be fired, and which demanded only attendance, not attention. You could say to a junior-college student, "If you don't want to learn, tough." But in elementary school you can't say that. You have to make them get it. An elementary school child is not in a position to decide if he or she should be educated. To allow children to decide whether or not to participate is tantamount to letting them decide whether or not to commit the murder of their own futures. I cared, so I struggled. Every day was a struggle. I strove to make mine a wonderful, interesting class but I

was continually fighting the lack of discipline. And why? Not the pay. Not the prestige. I knew I was in trouble when my boyfriend asked me why I stayed in teaching and all I could say was because I have a degree in it.

Despite her recognition of the shortcomings of her career, Ginger could not bring herself to quit; instead, she cried. "Virtually every night as I recalled the day, I would break into tears." Ginger's future was part of her agony; She admitted to herself the woeful constancy of a job that was like the seasons—always changing but always the same.

Ginger almost came to accept her hopelessness, but compromised; she attempted to alter her position while remaining a teacher. She earned her master's degree and took a position as a reading specialist. If Ginger's decision had been that teaching was basically rewarding, altering the kind of teaching she did might have worked, she might have been happier in her job. Sadly, however, Ginger had concluded that teaching was profoundly unsatisfying, and her new position was only a compromise, a fresh horse down the wrong trail.

> I went from being an unhappy teacher to being an unhappy reading specialist. Big deal. I was still frustrated and very angry. One little incident finally broke me. It came early in my fourth year and was not extraordinary in and of itself, but it was what pushed me to a decision. This little child, a female, decided that she was not going to stand in line with the other children, she was going inside. I told her three times to get back in line. Each time she said, "I ain't gonna." You know how that would grate on a teacher. We were not permitted any physical force with the children, so I could only repeat myself. Finally, she took her bucket—all the children had these buckets to carry their books and pencils—and she threw her books at me. I yelled and screamed, and she yelled and screamed, and I finally took her little hand and marched her to the principal's office. He listened to me, then told me to just take the girl and go on back to class. I said, "No. I am not

going to just let her get away with this. Her parents must be told, and she must be sent home for the day." He refused, so I yelled and screamed at him too. I ended up calling the parents myself—doing his job—and telling them to come get their daughter and take her home.

That was it. My teaching career was over, although I finished out my contract.

Ginger's contract specified eight more months of teaching, months Ginger put to use in a lengthy preparation for a new career. Her first step was to begin the physical preparations for a possible drop in salary or a spell of unemployment. Ginger took the small but determined step of arranging for automatic salary deductions to go into a savings account. She set a goal for herself of enough cash by the end of the school year to support her for three months. Toward the end of the year Ginger also took on a roommate to help reduce her living expenses, for she feared that a new job would be slow in coming. Fellow teachers had held a running dialogue on alternative careers; since none of the talkers had actually quit teaching, the conversation was dour, pessimistic. Ginger's first attempts to find places to apply for a job induced her to join the bleat. Yet she was indomitable, having known hopelessness, "whether" was no issue, only "where." Further, Ginger was financially prepared for months without work. She was fortified for the transition.

Unemployment is the great impetus to an effective job search, not merely in the obvious sense of hunger's prodding or even in the time and freedom joblessness affords, but also in the way friends and even friends of friends begin to listen for openings—two ears become twenty the day someone resigns. Ginger did not have a single solid job lead on the day she turned in her contract renewal unsigned. Within two weeks of announcing her decision to resign, she had one job offer and six solid possibilities. She diligently pursued them all, and by the day she walked away from her classroom, she had accepted an administrative position with the junior-college district.

The Case in Perspective

Once Ginger had accepted the hopelessness of her teaching

career, she was able to make her decision to quit and to begin
preparations to exit smiling. Other than her financial readiness,
her preparations were unsuccessful. The prospects for a new
career were woeful until the end of the school year, eight
months after her decision. If Ginger's quitting had depended on
the success of her implementation strategy, she would have remained in teaching, broken and uninterested. But Ginger had
made a decision without considering how she would implement
it, and she had no reason to be dissuaded from her new course
simply because the future was uncertain; in teaching, her future
was certain and unwanted, incapable of beckoning her. Again,
implementation was not related to success.

READY OR NOT

The last great decision of a career—sometimes the only great
decision of a career—is when to leave. When the decision is to
retire, it is the last quit. So often, of course, it has not been a
decision: Happy sixty-fifth birthday and good-bye. Now, Gray
Panthers and all, the retirement question is becoming once again
a genuine decision, a true quitting decision.

Franklin had plenty of time to think about his future in the
office supply business—twenty-two years from the time he first
considered retiring. For the last four of those twenty-two years
Franklin had seen the uncompromising sameness of his future;
he was sales manager and would be sales manager until the day
he collapsed onto his desk calendar. He would be replaced only
over his dead body, promoted over the dead body of the vice
president (two years younger). At age fifty-five, Franklin decided he had had enough of office supplies. He was ready to
reassert his vitality, ready to enjoy life, ready to retire.

> Our company had experienced a tremendous growth in
> the early 1970s—we just tried to keep up with it. Expenses
> didn't matter because the revenues were so very, very
> strong. Boy, we were sure smart in the early seventies.
> Then, of course, the economy wasn't so great anymore,
> and we weren't quite so smart all of a sudden. That's
> when all the trouble started. We couldn't afford to make

mistakes, and yet the quality of the help seemed to just drop off. In our industry we just couldn't go on with mistakes—wrong shipments, no quality control—the salesmen got very frustrated. Basically, to be candid, the job went from pleasant to a pain in the ass. When I saw that I wasn't enjoying what I was doing, I knew that I wanted to retire.

When Franklin shared his decision to retire with his family, they were annoyed, even resentful; Franklin's wife, Dottie, declared she would not be able to stand having Franklin underfoot all day; Franklin's son reminded his father that he had two more years of graduate school and a promise of financial support.

When I was eighteen I took my first full-time job. The longest I've been away from work in any of these thirty-seven years is two weeks. For a third or half of those years I also held down a part-time job, selling suits at Penney's or doing some other lousy job that would give us a few extra bucks for the couch or the car or whatever it was we needed at the time. My kid and my wife got spoiled—so I told them it was their turn to support me.

Franklin asserted his Self-interest but did not make a Clean Decision; being a practical man, he needed to plan his implementation and his future.

I started to collect all the facts about my financial position should I leave the company. One thing I learned was that the agreement for the pension fund and the other money I had accumulated at the company had some stipulations, including a one-year notification of intent to retire. That meant that I couldn't do anything precipitously, which relieved my family.

I also learned that the amount of money I would get by retiring at fifty-five was much less than what I could get at age sixty-two, which was still less than at sixty-five. That wasn't a surprise, of course; the surprise was how little the monthly amount seemed. The last time I had looked at the numbers, it seemed like it would be plenty, and then suddenly it didn't seem like plenty. My son had two or three years of school left to become a dentist, and I saw right away that I would have to wait until he was finished. But even after he was gone, there was such a heavy penalty for retiring early, and I naturally had some hesitation along the lines of, "What am I going to do with all that time on my hands?" and "What if I don't like it?" So I knew I had to wait.

Each year on his birthday Franklin would review the finances of retirement to see if he could afford to quit.

What was most disheartening was my savings. I had started a savings plan ten or twelve years before I first hit retirement age. When I had planned that savings, I was going to have, I think it was, over twenty thousand dollars saved by the time I was sixty. When I had started, that was a vast sum. By the time I was sixty, I was glad to have it, but it wasn't Big Money like I planned. If I had retired early, it would have been gone in five years. I was hoping to live twenty-five more years. I might make it, in fact.

Franklin finally retired at age sixty-two—seven years after his decision to try to retire. Although he was held hostage to his work by his financial future and his desire to maintain his living standard during retirement, he did not simply await the end in gloomy contemplation on the unfairness of life. In addition to the careful financial reviews every year, he began to prepare for retirement and for the transition from devoted worker to devoted nonworker.

When I saw that I couldn't retire in my fifties, I was a little resentful. I thought I had it coming to me to be able to retire. Anyhow, I decided I was going to live that much longer. I began to say to myself, "Frank, you take better care of yourself; you got to live an extra seven years." I knew that during the last couple of years of work I had to slow down. I'd been a conscientious, hard worker, and I tried to stay gung ho, but I made up my mind to live longer and live better by slowing down. I wouldn't leave the house in the morning until 9:30 or 10:00. Sometimes I'd come home for lunch, and I started leaving work before 6:00. I was preparing myself for retirement.

Franklin also took up a new hobby and learned how to do some of the household repairwork he had always avoided. "Everybody said I would never retire," Franklin remembers, but on his sixty-second birthday he walked away.

The Case in Perspective

Perhaps the financially motivated delay in Franklin's retirement was beneficial, for few men are as well prepared for retirement as he was: Franklin had made careful financial arrangements and had succeeded in readjusting his energy level to prepare thoroughly for endurance enjoyment. He was able to leave his company without the slightest remorse and experienced almost immediate adjustment to his new life. (Even Dottie, his wife, had the time to accept the idea of his weekday presence.) In sum, it was both a successful quit and a successful implementation.

ILLUSIONS

The enchanting premise of Richard Bach's *Illusions* is that Donald Shimoda is an airplane mechanic and the latest Messiah (miracles, epigrammatic wisdom, and all) who does not want the latter job and claims he is resigning. Donald seeks to recruit Richard, a pilot and the other main character, to be a messiah also. In the early part of the book, Richard, still an ordinary mortal, is puzzled by the Mechanic Messiah and particularly his desire to give up messiahing. "I didn't know the Messiah could just turn in his keys like that and quit." Richard is told

> "Of course you can quit! Quit anything you want, if you change your mind about doing it. You can quit breathing, if you want to," He floated a Phillips screwdriver for his own amusement. "So I quit being the Messiah, and if I sound a little defensive, it's maybe because I am still a little defensive. Better that than keeping the job and hating it.

A good messiah hates nothing and is free to walk any path he wants to walk. Well, that's true for everybody, of course."

So we are told, and by the Messiah at that. Yet quitting is so divinely difficult that the Messiah cannot follow his own defensive proclamation. Naturally, like any good Messiah, this one cannot bear to see all the suffering Someone put in the world and cannot resist an occasional healing. This attracts crowds, which, Richard (the mortal) recognizes as dangerous. Richard decides to quit his friendship with Donald, the Messiah, but, like Donald, he cannot just leave.

"We are all free to do whatever we want to do," he said that night. "Isn't that simple and clean and clear? Isn't that a great way to run a universe?"

So the Messiah who cannot quit tells the apprentice Messiah who cannot leave. When the apprentice Messiah objects to his mentor's assertion and protests that "as long as we don't hurt somebody else" be added to Donald's summary on running the universe, the Messiah produces a vampire in need of human blood, who insists that unless the apprentice allow his blood to be sucked, the vampire will die. When the apprentice refuses, he, and we, are shown that by trying never to hurt another individual we relinquish control over our own lives, permitting anyone who says, "I'll be hurt if you do (or don't)" to lead us, control us, manipulate us. Then follows advice worthy of a Messiah: "We choose, ourselves, to be hurt or not to be hurt, no matter what." Never to hurt a partner is quite impossible; to try is to yield all control to another—to some other who decides what does and does not hurt. "You'll hurt me if you do," becomes a loaded gun that the person about to be left presses to his own temple: interpersonal terrorism.

Although "You'll hurt me," whether spoken or unspoken, is often the obstacle to be overcome in implementing a quit, hurting was not the obstacle to Donald Shimoda's quitting his messiahship; even after Shimoda had his sense of hopelessness for his role as Messiah and even after he had asserted his Self-interest, he still lingered: He simply appeared loath to give up his powers as Messiah. One cannot *successfully* quit until one quits. Since he was a Messiah, we are to treat his actions like the words of a poet—assume deep meaning and search until an explanation is found. If we grant the mechanic this treatment, we can assume that he was merely stalling until his mission to train his friend in messiahing was completed—the outwardly patient Messiah living out his duty; inside, itching to go. Indeed, this Messiah does arrange for his own abrupt murder and at last has a Clean Break quit.

Illusions in Perspective

Richard Bach's fascinating character, the Mechanic Messiah, provides three lessons about quitting: (1) hurting another person cannot be the only criterion for life decisions—such a criterion entrusts all decisions to another, gives a life away; (2) a successful quit requires leaving; and (3) quit only when the mission is complete (hopelessness is a form of completion).

THE IRREVERSIBLE QUIT

Oh, those boys in the Mafia, always clowning around, always some new shenanigans. Whether it's a "banana race," a "cooler," some "juice" or a "serious headache," there's always something going on.

Definitions of the phrases quoted above are in *My Life in the Mafia*, the memoirs of Vincent Teresa, "a top Mafia thief, a mobster, and at times a brutal enforcer." In order, they are: a fixed horse race, a stacked deck of cards, loan-shark interest, and a bullet in the head. Never a dull moment.

A decision to quit a lucrative career is always difficult, but leaving the Mafia and becoming an informer takes a rare man; Teresa is said to be the highest-ranking Mafia figure ever to turn informer (he was the number-three man in the New England crime family). When he quit, "the mob offered five hundred thousand dollars to anyone who can find and kill him." Clearly, it is an understatement to say that it must have been a difficult decision for Teresa; however, like those with more ordinary quitting decisions to make, Teresa was helped when he recognized the hopelessness of his career.

Teresa's career was one of such seamy pursuits as the Gillette Razor heists. A warehouseman who had accumulated debts to loan sharks was allowed to work off his debts by loading ten or twelve cases of razor blades into a truck each week; the blades were then resold to drugstores or supermarkets. The store owners got merchandise at a large discount and asked no questions: "I think that's one reason why it's almost impossible to kill the mob," says Teresa. "They grow and thrive because they use the greed of the average guy, the businessman in particular." The petty heist of razor blades became big business when Gillette decided to market a new type of blade. Two truckloads of the outdated blades were sent to a salvage company to be hauled out to sea and dumped; but Teresa went to the owner of the salvage company and offered to buy the blades, millions of them, at a half cent a blade. The salvage company owner got paid both by Gillette and by Teresa, and Teresa sold the repackaged blades for two and a half cents apiece—a 500-percent gain.

While the victims of Teresa's greed were often distant and unaware, such as the Gillette Corporation, Teresa was finally caught and accused by his partners, other crime figures seeking to avoid prosecution. A stock swindle came apart, and two other swindlers made "deals with the feds to keep their own skirts clean." Teresa went to trial and, despite his efforts to "con the jury," was found guilty. He described his emotions:

> Now the panic was on. I faced twenty years in jail, and I had two other cases hanging over my head in state courts, not to mention lawyers demanding more money to handle the appeal. I took a good look at everything, and I realized I was in a real jam. I didn't have any money, to speak of, salted away for the family. There was about three hundred grand in cash in a safety deposit box . . . but I wanted a helluva lot more so that my family would live in comfort while I did my time.

Teresa's appeal failed in the sense that he was convicted and given a twenty-year sentence, but the appeal afforded him the time to initiate another securities swindle, to invest in land, and to make other deals with a potential twenty-million-dollar return—or rather, afforded Teresa almost enough time. His bail was revoked before he could bring in his profits. Because he was in prison when the deals were concluded, his partner simply kept all the proceeds. To add to Teresa's problems, another of his former associates panicked and was given federal protection before Teresa could have him "whacked out"—killed. Even the cash in the safe deposit box was cleaned out by one of Teresa's partners. Teresa's family was threatened. The wolves turned on the pack leader in the trap.

Although Teresa had turned "sour" on the mob, and he feared for his family, it was not until yet another betrayal that he admitted hopelessness and began to search for alternatives to his failed Mafia career. Teresa might have been content to sit out his sentence—he said that he enjoyed his prison work of picking up trash using a stick with a nail in the end—and he had a number of friends in prison, but when Teresa learned that he was to be tried for a bank swindle and his partners were lining up to testify against him ("a stacked deck for the trial," the former gambler called it, shocked and offended) he was so angry that he began to investigate new alternatives. One of them was turning State's evidence in exchange for immunity.

Teresa turned informer and claims he is responsible for twenty-seven convictions against twenty-one criminals and for indictments pending against twenty-seven others. To turn informer and therefore rate a five-hundred-thousand-dollar price on one's head is to implement a decision by means of a Clean Break. Before the Mafia found out that he was quitting, Teresa and the government personnel assigned to protect him had to plan a complete safety program. Teresa's family was "scooped up" and moved and permitted no communication with friends or relatives. The federal government supported them (seven hundred dollars a month), and an FBI agent checked on them every day. Teresa was given a reduced sentence and moved to a comfortable cell next to that of Joe Valachi, who became a pal.

Teresa now says that the only thing he misses about the mob "is the money." He prefers "straight" people to mob people; he feels less pressure and is closer to his family. He says,

Now I see that I wasted the best years of my life. You never retire from the Mafia; you either die or hide. But until they find me, I'm going to enjoy my life with my family.

Vincent Teresa in Perspective

Vincent Teresa's story is one of a successful quit. Despite years in prison, the constant fear of discovery after being released, the loss of all previous friendships, and the absence of a career—in sum, despite a painful fall from the heights of power and wealth—Teresa does not look back with regret, save for the regret that he did not exit sooner. A clear vision of his future had he chosen to remain loyal makes his decision self-evident, and thus, looking back, he is free from self-doubt and remorse.

Teresa's is a useful story of implementing a quit in that it illustrates an effective Clean Break. In Teresa's case, only a Clean Break could have succeeded. Any open preparations, confrontations, or half steps would have resulted in his death or that of a member of his family. Having reached hopelessness and the clean decision that followed, Teresa was virtually certain of achieving success, but only if he could make it happen with a successful implementation.

THE IMPLEMENTATION IN PERSPECTIVE

Anyone who has observed a nest of fledgings has seen the endless stretching and flapping of young wings, the seemingly indispensable readying for flight. How surprising it is to learn that that preparation is unnecessary: A biologist placed a group of young birds in tubes that prevented wing movement; once the tube babies matured, they were quite able to fly, without practice. So it is with the quitter; the preparation that seems so invaluable is not. Fly from the nest. The maturity, not the practice, counts.

VII

ADVICE

AND OTHER

DICE

ADVICE. The impending end of a relationship draws it the way a wedding draws presents. And like a wedding gift, the advice may not match, may be difficult to return, may be expensive *and* in bad taste; but whatever the value, grateful acceptance is expected, even demanded.

Valueless advice is pumped through the body of a dying relationship. It is embalming fluid imparting an illusion of life and health: She looks so natural, as if only sleeping; dead inside, smiling outside.

A review of a handful of previous cases shows how valueless advice has served to keep vain hope alive by imparting the myth of transcendence:

- Viola Kerns sought the advice of anyone, everyone, to save her marriage. The advice she got: This too shall pass. Twenty-five years Viola waited for the passing. Now her belief is that professional counseling exacerbated her conflicts by bringing out her dissatisfactions without encouraging action.

- When Donna Byron was contemplating abandoning her teaching career, her mother told her not to be a "ninny." Donna spent nine years not being a ninny, and not being happy. She quit and discovered that she had wasted nine years.

- Wilson Meredith left two successful careers—one in music, one in engineering—over the protests of friends and relatives. He was labeled a malcontent and worse, but he courageously made up his own mind about the suitability of each career.

- Kat listened first to her conscience—the ghost of advice past—then to a minister, then a psychiatrist: All advised patience and perseverance. Her suppressed rage caused violence and eventually the inevitable, divorce.

- Margaret Trudeau believed the guru who told her "all thought leads to sorrow" and set her upon a thoughtless, reckless course of action that led inexorably to sorrow.

- Father Tim received so much advice about ridding his life of temptation that he needed a convoluted rationalization for leaving the priesthood in order to pursue his happiness.

No shortage of bad advice. If advice was monolithically wrong, it would be a reliable predictor of success: See where the majority points and run the other way. But, naturally, some advice does turn out to have been correct.

- John Dean was persuaded by his lawyer to go to the prosecutors before he could be made the villain for Watergate.

- Emma went into a hospital so she would have time to contemplate her options for her uncontrollable daughter. Not only the hospital's therapy but her husband's counsel helped her to a correct decision.

- Stephen's visit to two lawyers was able to save him from entering a career for which he was not intended. The lawyer's descriptions of their profession served as indirect advice to ingenuous Stephen.

And, in addition to good advice and bad advice, there is no advice:

- Bill Russell's decision to retire from basketball was entirely private. Even once it was made, he did not share it with anyone for months.

- Mary quit her church and arranged to move to a new city rather than accept the reactions of her neighbors to her divorce. She kept her decision to seek a divorce a secret, especially from her husband, for eight years.

What is to be learned from the good advice and bad advice and nonadvice sprinkled throughout the cases of this research? The conclusion is the conspicuous absence of any relation between the success of a quit and the extent to which one consults others in making a decision. Consultation may be useful, but its usefulness is unpredictable. Any attempt to estimate where useful advice may come from is clearly doomed: Good advice, like bad advice, may arise anywhere.

Financial analysts and economists have an expression for events that are inconsistent and unpredictable: "It's a random walk." Advice, as the cases that follow will further demonstrate, is a random walk.

PROLONGED INFIDELITY

The first time Shari heard of her husband's infidelity, the news came from her best girl friend. Shari's husband, Bruce, an assistant professor at a small private college, had felt compelled to confess a not particularly romantic dalliance (a one-of-his-students, just-sex-no-strong-feelings affair) to Shari's best friend. Three degrees in history should have taught Bruce something more about human nature, for Shari heard the story within a week, and though the affair was over, Shari walked out on Bruce within an hour of receiving the unwelcome news of his brief enchantment.

Shari was eventually placated; being a disciplined Catholic, her abhorrence of adultry was finally tempered by her abhorrence of divorce. She forgave, but did not forget.

When I left the first time, he was shocked that I would go. "What did I do wrong?" he kept asking. He couldn't

understand that something that was in the past could affect me so much in the present. But I had learned about it
in the present, and it said a lot to me about his character,
and I lost some respect for him. I was naïve. I was not
used to being deceived. Because divorce was out of the
question—nobody in my family had ever been
divorced—I forced myself to agree that I was making too
much out of the whole affair. I found out just a couple of
days before Thanksgiving, and I either had to make a
scene and let both families in on our problem or I had to
move back in. I moved back.

Sharing failure is an intimate experience; pain attracts the
comfort of human closeness, even between the hurt and the
hurter; Shari and Bruce each needed solace and warmth, and
each could turn only to the other. The healing of the first break
seemed to make the relationship stronger than the original
union. However, within a year Bruce had developed a set of
faculty friends who kept him away from home with increasing
regularity. Shari knew that something was wrong. She had no
physical evidence—no lipstick on the collar or panties in the back
seat—but a decline in Bruce's sexual "demands" and her intui-
tion led her to suspect infidelity. Shari's best friend (the same
one who broke the story of the first affair) was enlisted to assist
in some rudimentary spying. Shari and her friend set up a
stakeout across from the college, followed Bruce to a bar after he
left the campus, then to a suburban home. Stealthily the two
located a side window to the living room. Bruce sat on the couch
watching television and eating popcorn with a fellow instructor,
a "homely but large-busted woman," curled at his side. The
casual intimacy of their touches and words was as convincing as
having caught them *in flagrante delicto*.

I went wild when I saw them. My friend had her arms
locked around me and sort of dragged me to the car. She
told me she wouldn't let me go to the door until I calmed
down. I drove us back to my apartment and packed. I was
moving out. After I had packed, I said that I was calm,
and we drove back.

I went to the door and told that woman that I wanted to
see my husband. She said that he wasn't there. I said that
he was and I pushed past her. He wasn't in the living
room, so I started opening bedrooms and closets while
she cursed me. Finally I found my husband in the bathroom. He started to give me a nonchalant routine, but I
cut him off and announced that I was moving.

Shari had made a decision to quit. Aided and abetted by her
closest friend, she moved, then consulted an attorney on divorce
proceedings. When Bruce's parents, with whom Shari was very
close, heard, they called to ask Shari to come talk with them.
Bruce's father sought to persuade Shari to give Bruce another
chance.

> His father really pressured me to go back to Bruce. This
> [her father-in-law] is a man I love and respect and did not
> want to disappoint, but I told him I could not go back to
> our house ever again. He explained that since Bruce was
> starting a big research project, he was going to change
> and that Bruce had promised them he would never even
> give the impression that he had been playing around
> again. His parents still thought he was innocent, I guess,
> and didn't know about the first time I'd caught Bruce.
>
> His father insisted, and I cried and said no, but then his
> father came up with a new proposal: Bruce and I would
> move in with them [Bruce's parents] for a while. Bruce
> and I could save some money for the new house we
> wanted, and they would help us patch together our mar-
> riage.
>
> I do love his parents, so I said I'd try.

The father, critically uninformed about his son's actual behavior, nonetheless pressed his advice upon Shari. She and
Bruce moved in. In doing so, Shari ignored the advice of her
best friend, who said "forget him."

The advice Shari received showed genuine concern but naturally tended to reflect the experiences of the one giving it:
Shari's best friend had been divorced and harbored endless sus-

picions; Bruce's parents had been married nearly thirty years
and believed in accommodation and endless compromise. The
advice Shari received from each turned out to be both right and
wrong.

Shari's friend insisted that to move in with Bruce's parents was
pointless—the arguing would merely spread to include the parents and worsen the problem. She was wrong. Shari calls the
year spent with her in-laws "one of the best years of my life, and
the best year of our marriage, by far." By the end of that pacific
year, Bruce and Shari bought a house of their own. It was the
parents' turn to be wrong—about Bruce.

> We had a really strong marriage at that point. Then I
> don't know what happened. I mean it happened again.
> Bruce was teaching a night class at that time. One night I
> was out to dinner with my friend, the same friend again,
> and I suggested that we stop by the college and say hello
> to Bruce. We were near the school, and it was just after
> the end of his class. I wasn't checking up on him, I just
> wanted to say hello. We had trouble finding him, but we
> saw him in the gymnasium. This girl was there. They
> were just standing together, but they both acted real ner-
> vous. She got out of there, fast. I was suspicious but didn't
> say anything. My friend and I left, but she talked me into
> parking up the hill so that we could overlook the parking
> lot. Bruce came out with the girl, and they drove off to-
> gether.

Shari again packed her suitcases. The first time she moved,
Bruce had persuaded her to return. The second time, Bruce's
father had done the persuading. This time Bruce convinced her.

> Bruce was adamant against a divorce. He apparently
> wasn't overly hot on marriage, but he didn't want a di-
> vorce. He told me he needed some time and that if I came
> back and he ever was unfaithful again, I could take every-
> thing and leave him. I had to find out for sure that it was
> the right thing for me, to leave him, so I moved back.

The last bargaining chip of the one to be left behind is the promise of a simple, mutually agreed-upon end. The price asked for that chip is to give up the end—to give, over and over, the One More Chance. To offer a painless quit is easy and nonbinding—a cheap offering, but one with great appeal to a hesitant, diffident quitter. Without the benefit of a Clean Decision, Shari was vulnerable to persuasion. Without an assertion of Self-interest, Shari was unable to attain a Clean Decision.

> He was supposedly straightening up his act, but apparently he was seeing the girl I'd seen at the gym all along. She even called the house. The final straw came at Thanksgiving—I hate Thanksgiving; it always brings bad things. A friend of Bruce's called to tell me that Bruce was at the women's dorm seeing that girl. "They're together right now," he said. I packed all my stuff and left. And that was it.

But that was not "it." Shari was to be persuaded one more time. She was finally able to resist the pleas for another chance, but she was susceptible to a final stalling tactic—the Counselor. Like One More Chance, the Counselor is a suggestion, a plea, and an argument—"You can quit, but not until , , ." The logic of "professional guidance" is difficult to refute. Be reasonable. Don't shoot the dog until you're sure it's dead.

The counselor was in a position to do an autopsy, perhaps a faith healing, but not to provide a solution; Shari's marriage was terminal before "help" was sought. Given the nature of the counseling sessions, an earlier start would not have mattered.

> We went to this marriage counselor, and when we were there, it was suddenly all my fault. My husband set an atmosphere of "What can we do about *her* problem?" Because I said I wanted a divorce and my husband didn't, I was the bad guy. I felt like one of those rape victims on trial—I'd been abused, but everyone was attacking *my* character, while the man sits there looking serious. And my husband put up this innocent act the whole time. After a while the counselor started to act like we were

both crazy. I'd tell him one thing, and my husband would tell him something just the opposite. The counselor started to act like the whole problem was ridiculous. He just stared at us and gave us weird looks. He didn't give us any feedback. He just stared. Finally I refused to go to him.

Confused and weary, Shari added to the confusion by asking for still more advice; she sought the opinion of her Catholic priest. He suggested an annulment.

Shari continued to receive the prescriptions and proposals of both her family and Bruce's and of their friends. At last, through the cacophony of guidance, Shari screamed inwardly, "No more!" She finally made up her mind that the decision was hers alone. She asserted her Self-interest and made a Clean Decision to quit.

The Case in Perspective

Shari's was a successful quit after an agonizingly protracted refusal to decide. Shari depended too much on advice, was too willing to compromise, to be able to end her marriage efficiently. Shari was correct not to have quit until she could assert her Self-interest and make a Clean Decision; a critical function of the assertion of Self-interest is to objectify advice, removing the emotional bias of those giving it, turning opinions into information to be used or ignored in the decision. It is unfortunate that all the advice Shari got forestalled her Self-interest and added several unhappy years to a fated relationship.

HUMAN SACRIFICE

In *Candide*, Voltaire presents a memorable scene of a starving Candide searching for food: Candide asks a man who has just concluded a homily on Charity to share his bread.

> "My friend," said the orator to Candide, "do you believe that the Pope is antichrist?"
>
> "I have never heard that before," replied Candide; "but whether he is or not, I have no bread."

Candide encountered the same insistence on the wrong issue
that two hundred years later is still frustrating individuals seeking sustenance for a troubled relationship. While the mind is
lectured, the body dies. So it was with the dying marriage of a
modern Candide, who, influenced by a Pangloss of today, a
Counselor, sought help for a destructive marriage and was offered only the wistful philosophy of transcendence.

This modern Candide had fallen deeply, purposefully in love
shortly after reading *The Art of Loving*. His bride was given to
despondency and was often bellicose, but Candide and his bride
both loved James Taylor songs and hated college, and Candide
fell in love. Naturally, they married. Naturally, they were married in an outdoor ceremony in California, written by Candide.

Candide thought it unusual that his new bride seemed so unhappy. He brought her gifts and wrote her poems. He tried
singing her songs, but his voice gave her a headache, so he
stopped. Although she would brighten for a few days, she
seemed always to return to her melancholia. "Maybe we need a
change of scenery," she said. So Candide found a job in another
city. The new city was no help. "Maybe I need a job," she said.
He helped her find a job, but that only seemed to make her
worse. He turned to his bride's friends for advice. "She's always
been that way," they said. Candide knew he would have to teach
his wife the secrets of happiness he had learned. He shared with
her the worn paperbacks he cherished. They, too, gave her a
headache.

At last Candide despaired. Believing in God and man, he
prayed for divine assistance. Even this failed to brighten his sad
bride. "Who do you turn to when God has let you down?" Candide asked a friend. The friend told him of Dr. Pangloss, a
marriage counselor, the greatest in California and consequently
the greatest in the world. Candide wished to study the wisdom of
the great Pangloss but blushed to visit the wise man with his
small problems.

But the bride worsened, refused to eat, awoke shivering in the
warm nights, and by and by, Candide sought an audience for his
bride with the great Pangloss. Candide had to solicitously lead
his wife, blinded by her own tears, to the Formica tower where

Pangloss received his patients. They waited a long while in a receiving room, distracted from their own worries by imaginings: "What bizarre consequences brought these outwardly ordinary people to see the virtuous Pangloss?" When they met the Doctor, he took Candide's hand and his wife's hand and held them in his own. From inside his silver beard came soothing words. From behind his glasses came reassurance. Pangloss sat very close to them and said that they would wait for the bride to finish her cry before talking. She cried a good time. Pangloss did not mind. He smiled, and Candide hoped.

Pangloss finally spoke: "There is no problem that you are not capable of solving. The world is the world. You are you, and she is she. All is well. You will learn that all is as it should be. Do you believe me?" Candide nodded vigorously: He had come to learn, not argue. "How about you?" he asked the bride. "I am not sure I believe anything," she said. This made Candide feel very bad, but it did not bother the more understanding Pangloss. "Very well. The sunshine is warmer on the face of one who looked for clouds." Candide shivered in the presence of such a man.

Pangloss at last let go of their hands. Candide worried that he had sweat on the Doctor, but Pangloss would not be affected by such concerns, Candide told himself. Pangloss instructed Candide to speak. He told his story. Pangloss instructed the bride to tell her story. She tried, but was twice stopped by her copious tears. Pangloss offered his handkerchief. Candide was upset when his bride, obviously crazed by her worries, blew her nose on the Doctor's handkerchief. Pangloss showed no emotion even at the violation of his handkerchief, but nodded with sympathy and held his eyes in a half squint of apparent concentration. Nearly two hours passed in the telling and retelling of the bride's unhappiness. The bride concluded her tale. Pangloss again spoke: "No need for despair. I have heard you, and I will accept the case," he told Candide. To the bride, he said, "I will need to see you every afternoon for the next two weeks." To both he said, "Then I will decide how we shall proceed."

Candide left elated. His bride would be cured, he felt certain. She seemed already to be cheered. Candide thanked God that his prayer had been answered after all.

Candide's bride visited the Doctor each weekday, except on
Tuesdays, when he was not available to any patient. The bride
spoke not of her sessions, for Pangloss had cautioned her not to
share the story of their psychological journeys. His bride did not
seem much changed, but Candide hoped. When the postman
brought the first bill, in a lovely, reassuring envelope, Candide
was taken aback to know that the great Doctor received a dollar a
minute for his counseling, a dollar and a half a minute if a
session went over an hour. "Only prostitutes are paid so well,"
Candide said to no one and everyone, but he would not complain within the hearing of his bride, for she would tolerate no
criticism of the Doctor.

Soon Candide again despaired. He now had both a sick wife
and no money. His insurance company helped, but Pangloss
charged far more than the rules permitted. "I personally would
like to see the rule change," the smiling little old woman at the
insurance company told Candide, "but then the quacks would
suck our blood until we were dry. We wouldn't want that, would
we?" Candide commented on his being dry, and the woman
stopped smiling.

Candide could not even get his bride to tell him what she did
with Pangloss. She did announce that she would begin to see
Pangloss just twice a week; evidence of progress, she said.

Months later Pangloss declared that he would begin to counsel
with Candide as well. When Candide returned to the Formica
tower, Pangloss told him that all was well and that his wife was
progressing nicely. "But how can this be?" asked Candide. "She
is no different, except that now she complains about money
more often, as do I."

"This is why I chose to work with you," said Pangloss. He
moved his chair very close to Candide until their knees were in
constant danger of touching. "You must learn to accept your
wife."

"But she is unhappy. She is depressed. I cannot be jocular in
the face of such."

"Life is more than laughs. You must learn to be happy with
your wife as she is and is not. Do not be distressed, I will teach
you all you need to know. You have already the victory in your

heart. You must learn to embrace your victory, for it is yours. You have a perfect wife, and you are the perfect husband. I will show you where your perfection waits." Pangloss tapped his forehead, then his heart. "Do you believe me?" "I am not sure what I believe," replied a troubled Candide. "The sunshine," Pangloss said, "is always warmer on the face of the one who looked for clouds." "So I've heard," said Candide.

Candide and Pangloss spoke for a hundred and thirty dollars. Candide told himself that the money would have been better spent on a prostitute, then chided himself for such a thought. He did not understand, but followed his money to the great Pangloss twice a week. At last impatient, Candide asked Pangloss when he could expect some improvement in his wife. "How little you have learned, Candide," he said. "Your wife is perfect."

"But she is unhappy, and she makes me unhappy in her presence."

"Do not blame your wife for your unhappiness, Candide. You must learn to accept perfection as is."

Candide was quite upset and startled himself by demanding more of the Doctor. "Is there nothing I can do?"

Pangloss moved away from Candide and over to his desk, where he read a thick file for nearly twenty dollars. Finally, he looked hard at Candide and spoke: 'I resist handing out solutions, for the solution is within you, not within me. I do have a suggestion I have been saving for you and your wife, when you are ready. It will mean fulfillment of your life. I will tell you when you are ready."

Candide then made an earnest effort to be worthy of Pangloss's wisdom. He trained himself to stand logic on its head and to warm himself with the experience of what seemed his wife's depression. One day Pangloss told Candide that he was ready to fulfill his life. "You are a Christian, Candide?" "The generous would say yes," answered Candide.

"You undoubtedly know the unhappy home your wife experienced as a child. And you know how deeply she is capable of loving. And you are aware of her wishes to cease the pressures of her career and become a complete wife and a mother."

"All this I know, but—"

Pangloss raised his hand for silence. "Please, Candide, I am making a very important point." Candide sat back, nervous. "I am convinced," the Doctor continued, "that you and your wife should have a child. Your wife needs to reexperience childhood in a more supportive environment, and you need to fulfill your Christian duty."

Candide froze. He was alone but not frightened. Pangloss spoke on, but the words were trees falling in a distant wood. Candide rose, and as he did so he knew whom he would turn to when God had let him down. He legs felt sturdy under the weight of his determination. He left.

The Case in Perspective

The last words attributed to Pangloss were actually spoken by a financially successful psychologist still working in the Southwest. He genuinely believed the old theory that a child will save a failing marriage. Of course a child raises the stakes for quitting immeasurably, and undoubtedly succeeds in lashing two unhappy people firmly together, at least temporarily, but to suggest that a troubled marriage use a defenseless young human being as the glue for a broken vessel or the mask over an unsmiling face is blatant irresponsibility. Yet, fatuous advice, purchased at an exorbitant price, was woefully common in the cases where professional counseling was employed. Of the dozens of individuals interviewed (quitters and nonquitters alike) who had sought professional counseling, only one was convinced that the counseling had a distinguishable positive effect. Many, like the man called Candide above, left their counseling experience with a healthy mistrust. The Candide of this case left his Pangloss knowing that he alone could attain his happiness—which was the message Pangloss tried to impart—however, this Candide realized that he could find happiness not by acceptance but by change: He got a divorce and found happiness. Pangloss tried to teach Candide to live with the great pain in his heart. Candide learned instead to withdraw the knife that caused the pain.

THE POWER IS OUT

Burly but somehow approachable, with eyes that have seen much pain but somehow manage still to sparkle and a voice that always comes close to a chuckle—it is unimaginable that anyone would not immediately take to Roy Eugene, a trait that explains his success as a salesman of oil products. Yet Roy was not always a salesman, was not always as successful as he is today.

Roy began his career as an electrician's helper at a major private university. He rose slowly but steadily through the ranks: electrician, assistant foreman, foreman, assistant director of maintenance, and finally, assistant superintendent of maintenance and buildings. In his last position at the university, 108 men reported to Roy. "The school was good to me and gave me every opportunity, at least up to a point," Roy says. The point at which the opportunity ran out was the point of assistant superintendent, a position Roy held without promotion for nearly ten years. The workers Roy supervised were mostly black, and few shared Roy's dedication to providing America's wealthy WASP youths with flawless building and grounds maintenance. Until the sixties, Roy's blend of camaraderie, cajoling, and authority enabled him to attain a high level of performance, which satisfied the university and, a more difficult achievement, satisfied Roy. During the sixties influenced by the growing civil rights movement, the attitudes of his employees turned hard, less conciliatory. Although his work became less pleasant, Roy upheld his standards for performance until, abruptly, he lost his authority. In the midsixties the university initiated a personnel review committee before which any employee could take a grievance. The effect was to permit any employee a hearing before he could be fired. Roy was instructed that he was not to "lose a case"; that is, not to allow an employee to be in a position where the review committee would overturn Roy's decision. This meant Roy could fire an employee only when he had developed a *prima facie* case against that employee, with evidence not merely of incompetence but of intentional wrongdoing. Roy described the environment:

> It was one of those situations where we became so concerned about the rights of the employee that we had to leave the rights of the students and faculty waiting. I couldn't get the men to come to work and I couldn't let

one go. They could practically lie down in front of me and go to sleep, and there was nothing I could do. But that wasn't any excuse for me not to get the job done. I was still responsible. I would plan very little work for Mondays and Fridays, because as many as half of my men would be out. If a man was a particularly flagrant violator, I would start to build a file on him. I had to document any abuses, any warnings I gave, and any disciplinary action. Then when the matter came to the review committee—if I tried to fire the man—he could sit there and call me a liar, and there wasn't a thing I could do except hold onto the chair. What I'm saying is that you needed both evidence and some witnesses who were willing to go against one of their own. That's not easy. For the most part, I couldn't fire a man.

Roy became like a man dying of thirst in the middle of the ocean: many assistants but little assistance. The university had higher expectations than his employees had ambition, and Roy was in the middle. With ingenuity and the clever use of his reliable employees, Roy kept the university functioning. But Roy worked harder and got less accomplished. He lay awake at night trying to devise a way to accomplish all that needed to be done. For four years Roy worked more and more, worried more and more.

Roy's wife, not normally an assertive woman, came to the rescue. "Look at what you're doing to yourself," she insisted to Roy. This was the first time Roy had stopped worrying about the grass and the plumbing to worry about Roy.

My wife is the one who made me see what was happening. I was so busy with all the school's problems that I never thought about myself. She made me think about me. She never was one to complain, and it wasn't like my work was destroying my marriage or anything, she was just concerned about my well-being. She saw that I wasn't sleeping good and that my mind was preoccupied, but she wasn't worrying about herself, she was worrying about me.

Thus Roy had his Realization: His job had declined from something rewarding to something that was draining him. His wife saw it first, and now he knew it. But the school was his entire professional life. The university had been good to Roy. He hesitated. Although he had never had the opportunity to attend college as a full-time student, he considered it *his* college—he rarely missed a sporting event and was surrounded by friendships. But the old school was not loyal to Roy. A younger man, one with a college degree, was given a promotion; Roy, with greater seniority and more relevant experience, was bypassed. The university, Roy felt, fulfilled its own promise that a degree was important. Roy was at last ready to accept the hopelessness of his position: The job was, and would be monotonously unrewarding. Again his wife's loving prodding helped Roy to see the reality of his circumstances; she urged him not to be unselfish but rather to consider his own Self-interest, and she dragged him to a Clean Decision.

The Great Step for Roy was in the direction of a local photographer's studio, for a picture to put on his résumé—Roy's first step toward a new career. The résumé brought the polite iciness of form-letter refusals: The world was not waiting for a forty-year-old man who was leaving a rather high salary in a rather specialized field. Roy was discouraged. Again his wife urged him to persevere. Again she was right.

Nearly a year passed as Roy searched for an acceptable and accepting new career. The breakthrough in the search came when Roy, with the help of his wife, logically decided upon a career for which he had an aptitude and would enjoy the daily chores: sales. Roy was a natural raconteur and enjoyed physical activity; he was well suited for the role of manufacturer's representative. But Roy had no experience. With a chosen goal, he knew which direction he sought to travel in, and the obstacles became part of the journey. One of the suppliers to the university offered Roy a sales position, and despite Roy's certainty that the man's promises for advancement would not be fulfilled, he accepted the job.

> At that point I knew what I wanted, so I knew what I needed to learn and the type of experience I needed in

order to move into the sales position I really wanted. I began selling janitorial supplies, which I knew a great deal about from having worked in maintenance at the university. I had a lot of knowledge and experience, which helped me overcome my lack of sales experience. The job was a stepping stone.

Roy stepped from janitorial supplies into oil products and eventually became the sales manager for his company. He speaks with obvious fondness of the good times at the university but has the continuing reassurance of knowing that his career there was hopeless.

The Case in Perspective

Roy believes that it is only thanks to his wife that he is no longer toiling at a frustrating university job. She forced him to notice the decline in the satisfaction he got from his work and led him to the lonely Clean Decision. She did not urge Roy to act in her interest, but in his own. She encouraged a selfless man to act in his Self-interest. Further, she took part in analyzing alternative careers for him and supported her husband in the frightening step of surrendering fifteen years of pension contributions to take a short-term reduction in salary. Her advice, her willingness for sacrifice, and her love enabled Roy to make the first career change of his life. He needed her. And she never let him forget that she needed him . . . and needed him to be happy. She gave him confidence. He has repaid her well, with his own greater happiness.

MARJOE

His name is a contraction of the holy names of Mary and Joseph; his parents, although not waiting for a virgin birth, certainly wanted to raise a Christian son and a preacher. Marjoe Gortner was ordained at four. Until his adolescence he was a successful tent revivalist, exhorting crowds to fear hell and damnation and, less often, to know the joys of salvation. To the Fellini-esque scene of the rural revival—the portly, crude, red-faced men in overalls and the calloused farm women, the unkempt poor and the unfortunate ill, the lame and the deformed seeking a miracle, the twisted zealots, the children and the horses, all seen through the choking dust—was added the freakish performance of a child pastor screaming in a convincing parody of possession. A bizarre life for a jaded adult, a pathetic childhood.

Marjoe learned to shout "Glory" into a microphone at the age of nine months. By age eight Marjoe was healing his believers, even of blindness. (No man, or child, is a prophet in his own land, and Marjoe did not heal his own family—they preferred the more conventional ministrations of physicians.) At the age of twelve Marjoe lost his virginity. At thirteen he retired. From his biography *Marjoe*:

> Marjoe led his mother into the next room and seated her in a green-and-salmon-printed chair. He looked intently at her for a long time. Then he smiled. He spoke to her like a young man in total control of his life.
>
> "This is my last sermon, Mother. I'm quitting the business."
>
> "Don't be ridiculous, Marjoe. What would you do?"
>
> "I'd be a normal thirteen-year-old boy."

His mother's protests went unheeded, and Marjoe retired, although a child who had preached to over five million people could never quite go home to normalcy.

Marjoe's conviction to retire weakened at fourteen, and he was persuaded to do a revival in exchange for a new car for the family. Marjoe weakened again in his twenties; a young failure, he recalled his former glory and began to envision a comeback. The Miracle Child, as he had been billed, was back as an adult, with an adult, new message of love and peace. He preached for love and against the war in Southeast Asia. Following the first meeting he met with the minister who had arranged the resurrection of his career.

> "Marjoe, this is the worst offering we've received from the Lord in years. I don't think there's fifty dollars here." He hit the money with the back of his hand.
>
> "I can't understand it, Brother Lucas."

"I can." Lucas took a sip of bourbon. "Where's all that fire you used to have? What's all this peace and love nonsense have to do with church?"

Marjoe offered to change the following night's sermon but was told there were simply to be no more. His comeback had failed—or almost. A minister from Kokomo, Indiana, had been in the audience that night and offered Marjoe the chance to preach in his church.

The Kokomo crowd was described as "stoic." Marjoe sat "glumly," forced to listen to the sound of the devil laughing—change, not bills, falling into the collection plate. Marjoe was crestfallen. The kindly minister who had invited him to Kokomo was reassuring—the next night would be better. Marjoe agreed. The next night he would "give them what they want," a sermon in the old style. Marjoe's girl friend protested, begging him not to go back to the words he did not believe. "Don't lie to them," she pleaded. "I'm an entertainer," Marjoe told her. "I'm an entertainer for the Lord. I'm an evangelist, not a priest or a holy man. These people come to hear me to forget their miseries for a while, and I've got to give them their money's worth." She was persistent, and Marjoe relented. He preached his social gospel for two more nights. But when his girl friend then departed for home, Marjoe gave himself back to the old hellfire, say Hallelujah!

Marjoe, despite his girl friend's pleas, was back. She begged him to quit and return to her in Los Angeles. He was too good to quit, he told her. Even the black churches, which demanded the most in emotional preaching, wanted him. He reveled, enjoyed, was famous. With his renewed confidence the challenge faded, however. The drain on his "psychic force" was great. He discovered again that he was lonely, unhappy. Again he struggled with the decision to retire.

Marjoe's Clean Decision to quit came in Raleigh, North Carolina. A minister there was giving a sermon called "The Devil's Symphony," which would include the breaking of rock-music records. The congregation was invited to bring records forward to be broken over the minister's knee.

After the service, a young girl, who reminded Marjoe of his girl in Los Angeles, smiled at him and asked, "Is rock-and-roll really from the devil?" A young boy asked, "Will it really make us into drug addicts?" Marjoe could not answer. He bolted.

Marjoe in Perspective

Marjoe made his decision to retire at thirteen alone and in opposition to the wishes of his family. He made the decision to return to the revival circuit alone and in opposition to the wishes of his love. Finally, the questions of a young surrogate for his doubting girl friend were the impetus to his Clean Decision to retire. No one gave Marjoe unmistakable wisdom that became his decision; the first decisions were made in spite of advice to the contrary, the final decision to retire was made without advice. Marjoe ignored the urgings of the adults, finally to be forced to an insight by the questions of children. Advice, both good and bad, is omnipresent, for any word or deed (like the simple queries of children) can serve as the stimulus to the man ready to decide. The source of the advice is less important than the moment of receptiveness.

WILLIAM SLOANE COFFIN, JR.

While Marjoe Gortner was traveling the intellectual low road of American theological expression, William Sloane Coffin, Jr., was riding the high road, the chaplain at Yale and a visible civil rights and antiwar activist. In his memoir, *Once to Every Man*, Coffin recalls a story of the poet Heinrich Heine, who, when visiting the cathedral of Amiens was asked why people no longer build such great structures. Heine said the following:

> My dear friend, in those days people had convictions. We moderns have opinions, and it takes more than an opinion to build a cathedral.

Coffin makes light of opinions, but Coffin's life followed a consistent pattern of willingness to assimilate and act upon the counsel of friends. Perhaps humility leads Coffin to acknowledge his friends, or perhaps he is name dropping, for the advice seemed always to come from the famous, but Coffin repeatedly benefited from his friends' comments, although never seeming to invite their opinions.

When Coffin contemplated a divorce, Kingman Brewster told him of his own parents' divorce and offered to take him into his home. Rabbi Herschel later chided Coffin for not having leaned more upon his experience, telling him, "You Christians are so vexed by your perfectionism. It is always your undoing." Erik Erikson helped Coffin adjust to his divorce by speaking of Gandhi, who was "less than an ideal husband" ("refusing as a matter of principle to have sexual intercourse with his wife"). Coffin left his conversation with Erickson with this thought:

> While divorce certainly reflects a failure, the actual decision to divorce could be a sign of strength if it represents a refusal to remain passive in a destructive situation, and a sign of courage if taken in the face of considerable public opposition.

Despite the emotional upheavals in Coffin's life—the divorce, his arrest and trials related to his protesting—Yale was a sanctuary for Coffin, seemingly more so than his faith in God. But a sanctuary can be a base of strength or merely a hiding place; Coffin began to question his sanctuary.

Arthur Miller and Coffin, both living in or near New Haven, were together one January. Miller "suddenly interrupted his train of thought to blurt out, 'What the hell are we doing in Connecticut?' " Coffin had begun to ask himself the same question about Yale.

> I had often noted how in protecting free speech, in protecting professors from other people, tenure could also protect professors from themselves, from their further development. I didn't want my own tenure to do that to me. I wasn't sure what I would do were I not a university chaplain, but I was beginning to be convinced that personal growth demands a willingness to relinquish one's proficiencies.

But the step from Yale was too great for Coffin, and he could not leave. His departure had to await his own emotional hardening.

Trees prepare themselves for the winter by putting a layer of cork at the base of each stem; this cork chokes off the leaves, causing the tree to drop its foliage, but the tree is protected. Thus a man must prepare for the hard seasons of change. Coffin met with a disgruntled alumnus of Yale and used the conversation to teach himself a lesson.

> I thought I needed Yale to tell me who I was. It may be the most frightening thing about institutions of all kinds, that they have this kind of power over so many of us.

Later Coffin was influenced by a fellow pastor:

> As usual it took somebody else to draw from me my true feelings. . . . Joel Warren spent the night with us. A man of unusual bluntness, Joel wasted no time in going to work on me. "Coffin," he said, "what are you still doing here at Yale? This is maintenance, man, just maintenance."

Coffin explained that he was being responsible, not risking the security important to his children and wife (he had remarried). Coffin had no other job offer and no other source of income. But when asked, Coffin's family did not wish to be responsible for holding him back; they agreed to a change. Three weeks later, after seventeen years at Yale, Coffin had the courage to relinquish his proficiencies and resign.

William Sloane Coffin in Perspective

William Sloane Coffin seemed always to be surprised by the prescient words of his friends, forcing him to Realizations. He should not have been surprised, for wisdom and ignorance are always in the air. Coffin had to make himself ready to accept one or the other. The successful outcomes of his quits were not dependent upon the quality of the advice but upon the quality of his own preparation for quitting.

ADVICE IN PERSPECTIVE

Advice is like the sun: dazzling or barely noticeable, depending on how you look at it.

Advice is as plentiful as sunshine to the individual willing to take his or her problems outside. Those who have been burned often avoid advice, seeking an inner resolution to their decision. Such avoidance is typically associated with successful quitting, for those who avoid counsel have often accepted the necessity for deep commitment, for a Clean Decision with which they can live happily. However, the avoidance of advice may simply be an implicit acknowledgment of impulsive or irrational behavior.

Those who sought the warmth of counsel of friends or professionals are rarely ambivalent about the advice received; some credit their counselors with having driven them to an insight, many blame their counselors for having encouraged an incorrect decision or having postponed a correct decision.

The most common effect of counsel is to delay a quitting decision, for the advisors often offer "solutions" and/or reassurance. Many other individuals seek the opinions of a person whom they know will support an already imminent decision.

In sum, whether or not you receice advice and how much you receive prior to the quitting decision has no bearing on the eventual success of the quit. Advice is everywhere. A given individual may be benefited or harmed by it. Unlike the implementation of the quit, where the destination is significant but the nature of the journey is not, the path to the *decision* to quit does matter and is related to the eventual success of the quit. When advice helps a person to take a self-interested look at the quitting decision, or when the advice assists in a Clean Decision, it is valuable. When advice blurs the decision, clouds Self-interest, or places other obstacles in the path of a Clean Decision, it can postpone or prevent the healthy abandonment of a failed relationship. Thus, counsel is important only in its effect upon the key components of successful quitting; it is not directly related to success.

PUTTING THE PIECES

BACK TOGETHER

ROBERT BOLT's *A Man for All Seasons*, the story of Thomas More's conscience, re-creates More's trial for refusing an oath naming Henry VIII the Supreme Head of the Church in England (and, more generally, for refusing to support the king in his divorce of Catherine and his marriage to Anne Boleyn). More not only refuses the oath, he refuses any comment, hoping to take refuge in silence. During the trial Cromwell attacks this silence:

> Let us say it is the dead of the night—there's nothing like darkness for sharpening the ear; and we listen. What do we hear? Silence. What does it betoken, this silence? Nothing. This is silence, pure and simple. But consider another case. Suppose I were to draw a dagger from my sleeve and make to kill the prisoner with it, and suppose their lordships there, instead of crying out for me to stop or crying out for help to stop me, maintained their silence. That would betoken. So silence can, according to circumstances, speak.

Cromwell goes on to say that More's silence "was not silence at all but most eloquent denial," just as earlier he said that More's silence was "bellowing up and down Europe."

Silence can say everything or nothing. Absence of a relationship can betoken. So it is with the variables of quitting. Two of the variables that have no relation to success—advice and the implementation—have been explored at length; their silence—their *lack* of a pattern—was profound and therefore instructive. Six more variables not related to success remain. These too teach with their silence. They have both a role to play and a role *not* to play and should be considered. Rather than examining each in turn, the six variables will be examined in the context of four cases of quitting. The cases will of course include the six variables already examined as well, allowing them to serve as a summary of all the factors in quitting and the interaction of these factors.

Variables Related to Successful Quitting	**Variables with No Consistent Relationship to Success**
Futuring	Advice
The Realization	A Clean Quit (the
Self-interest	implementation)
The Clean Decision	* Time the relationship ran satisfactorily
	* Time to make the quitting decision
	* Time to implement a decision to quit
	* Presence of a "deadline" for a decision
	* Feelings on the day of decision
	* Feelings on the day of implementation

Not previously discussed.

TWICE IS ENOUGH

Rusty Keller twice faced down painful quitting situations: Her first quit was interestingly ordinary; her second, bizarre.

Rusty could well have asked the question Voltaire asks in *Candide*:

"I would like to know which is worse—to be raped a hundred times by Negro pirates, have a buttock cut off, run the gauntlet among the Bulgarians, be flogged and hanged in an auto-da-fé, be dissected, row in the galleys, in short to undergo all the miseries we have all been through—or to stay here doing nothing?" "It's a great question," said Candide. These remarks engendered new reflections, and Martin above all concluded that man was born to live in the convulsion of anxiety or the lethargy of boredom.

Rusty split her life between anxiety and lethargy. She says that her life has been *too* interesting; she has come to hate the boredom she has learned to prefer.

Twice Rusty has left a husband. She met and married her first husband when she was just sixteen years old.

> My childhood was bad. At sixteen I looked like I was twenty-one, but my mother treated me like a young child. Not only could I not date, I couldn't even pick out my own shoes. She wouldn't even let me pick the type of ice cream I wanted at the ice cream parlor. That's when I got married for the first time. He was a navy man. He was thirteen or fourteen years older. He was beautiful—he looked like Gene Kelly. And all the stars and stripes and all—you know—explosions and everything. I decided to marry him. Everyone said you're not going to do this, but I did. And I was unduly happy.

Rusty was "unduly" happy for three years, until her husband retired from the navy—no more stars, stripes, explosions. Her life settled into dreary routine. Rusty worked ten hours a day, then came home to prepare dinner and care for two children while "Gene Kelly" indulged in various get-rich-quick schemes.

> He absolutely, flatly refused to work. He was one of these men who answer those ads in the classifieds and put money into ridiculous ideas. He was one of the ones, for instance, to go out and get a metal detector and go out and try to find uranium and gold. I went back to work when my baby was four weeks old in order to feed us. And where is he when I come home from work? Sitting on the front porch in his nightshirt.

Although her marriage had begun promisingly, the promise had not been kept. Rusty's husband had retired from the navy, they had settled in California, and had had two children: They had entered a new phase of the marriage. Since the first phase of the marriage had been satisfactory, the second phase seemed likely to succeed. It did not. Rusty was no longer a little girl running away from home, and her husband was no longer in uniform. Two new people. A new toss of the coin. This time they were incompatible. This case illustrates how the length of time a relationship had been satisfactory prior to the first contemplation of quitting is not related to the success of the quit. The "smooth time" made the decision tougher; the decision process was thus lengthier, but the relationship being quit was quite different from that of the good times.

> Our marriage wasn't so hot. I sensed this and I suggested that we leave California and go back home to Illinois. He just said, "Damn Illinois." I tried to change, and that didn't help, and I tried to blame other people, and that didn't help. I told him how I felt about our marriage. He comes back later and tells me he knows what's wrong with our marriage—"Our sex life is dull," he tells me. He goes on to tell me he wants to see me make love to another man—he would bring somebody home for me. I told him he was crazy. He says to me, "Okay, then you pick the other man."

The "other man" conversation became Rusty's Realization, for before the conversation she sought change by changing; after the conversation she began to plan to change by leaving. She contemplated leaving and confessed to her husband her thoughts.

> He walked into the other room and picked up the phone and called my mother. He told her what I had said and told her to fly out to California and to talk some sense into me. That was incredible. But more incredible was that she came.

Shortly after her mother's unwelcome visit, Rusty awoke one morning determined to quit. Hers was a classic Clean Decision: "I just woke up and knew I really was going to leave him." The arrival of the Clean Decision—the decision of the jury of the subconscious—does not have any discernible estimated time of arrival. In outwardly similar quitting situations the inner deliberations can be set to exceedingly different clocks. These quit-clocks are perhaps related to the extent of the internalization of myths of transcendence or to childhood experiences with dislocation (parental separation or geographic relocation). The effect of these clocks is obvious in the rapidity of the Clean Decision following the Realization and assertion of Self-interest, but the formation and composition of the clocks is unclear, their speed unpredictable.

> One morning I got up to go to work and I looked at him across the table and said, "I'm going," and that was it as far as I was concerned. He told me he was going to call my mother again. I told him I had outgrown him and my mother. And I went to work.

Rusty should have given more consideration to the implementation of her decision to quit. Although the implementation is not related to success, a careful implementation would have brought Rusty her success far sooner, for when she returned from work she found her husband and children missing. It took two years to find them and another year for the legal proceedings to reunite her with her children. Her attempted implementation was too hasty, poorly planned.

Like the implementation of the quit, the time taken between the Clean Decision and the actual departure does have a relationship to the short-run ease of quitting, if not to eventual success. Although her implementation was overly swift, her quit was successful; the difficulties in locating her husband and reclaiming her "kidnapped" children convinced her of the wisdom of her decision while mocking her inept implementation.

Back in Illinois and still feeling cautious, Rusty chose her second husband. Still, in a way, a military man, he was a decorated veteran of the Korean war, but the second time, Rusty carefully

considered how compatible they were—yet the marriage eventually blew up in her face. Although she divorced her second
husband five years ago, her recollection of him brought tears.

> Believe it or not my eyes are running thinking about that
> crumb. I still love the man. I loved him more than any-
> thing else or anyone else in my life. He was the local hero
> in our town. Big football player. The one most likely to
> succeed. Medals. Just a super guy.

Superguy was discharged from the army and became a security guard back in his little town. He saved a child's life in a fire
and was, briefly, again a local hero. But the heroism of daily life
as a small-town guard was in surviving not bullets, but boredom.
Petty burglaries. Constant waiting for action that never seemed
to arrive . . . stalking Godot. He tried one or more affairs, then
liquor, searching for the lost excitement of his youth. Finally he
found more drama than he sought.

> Tommy was kinda experimenting with different things,
> but we had a basically sound marriage. My life was quiet
> and that was all right with me. I was working as an admin-
> istrative assistant to the president of our biggest depart-
> ment store. One day a detective came to the store and says
> he wanted to talk to me. The day before, a girl had been
> picked up on the street and then beaten and robbed. The
> detective asked me some questions and showed me this
> picture of a man and asked if he had been in my home
> recently, and I said no. Then he tells me they had ar-
> rested my husband, Tommy, that afternoon. He was in
> custody for having assaulted the girl. Naturally I just
> couldn't believe him. But it was true, and my world caved
> in.

Rusty had to sit through the trial, had to explain to the children that Daddy would not be home, had to face the small town
that knew.

> The whole county was only ten thousand people, and if I
> didn't know their name, they knew mine. I had been with
> the store for enough years that everyone in the county

knew me. If anybody pitied me, I'd just break down and cry, but if they left me alone, I could be very strong. It's a trait in me, I don't know why. But people would be kind to me, and I'd end up sitting at my desk with tears dripping off my chin.

Through the entire process of hearings and the trial my husband was convinced he would not be sent to prison. He believed all the stories the police tell each other, that criminals never go to prison. He was sentenced to prison for a minimum of four or five years before parole.

I was fortunate to have a very understanding employer who refused to accept my resignation and who treated me like a part of his family. I also had the children, so I was prepared to wait for my husband to pay for his mistake.

One of Rusty's functions as the administrative assistant to the store president was to make weekly deliveries of cash to the depository bank in the nearest city, eighty miles away. She drove with thousands of dollars in receipts as her passenger.

One day after I had made a delivery and had gone home for the day, Tommy's cousin showed up at the house, very upset. He told me that Tommy had worked out a plan for a second robbery and that I was the target. I told him I didn't believe him, but he went on to lay out all the details of the stretch of highway to run me off the road, the details he had been given about when and where I drove, how much I carried, and so on, and I knew that the information had to have come from Tommy. When Tommy's cousin had checked out Tommy's story, he saw that it was me in the car, and he immediately decided not to go through with it as soon as he saw me. Tommy had never told him who would be driving, but he had discussed the possibility of having to knock unconscious or even kill the driver—me!

Thus Rusty's had been the most dramatic Realization encountered in this research. But the Realization was too sudden to elicit true hopelessness; it did initiate some frenzied attempts to determine her husband's character.

> After his cousin came over, I decided to check with some
> mutual friends and see what my husband had been say-
> ing. I didn't want to believe what I had heard about him,
> but he was in prison and he had changed in the time he
> was in prison—it was two and a half years by then—and I
> had to find out. Two different friends told me he had
> made threatening remarks about me to them, because he
> was convinced I had been unfaithful to him. Apparently
> it's something that all prisoners fear, that their wives are
> running around. Tommy had asked his friends to spy on
> me and told them very seriously that he would have me
> killed if I fooled around.

Rusty confronted her husband with her knowledge. His reactions convinced her that he was guilty. She then experienced the
pain of hopelessness, asserted her Self-interest, and shortly
thereafter made a Clean Decision. Her decision made her weep,
for she had to bury a marriage that she did not want to die.
When she went to file for a divorce, her "legs were logs." When
the divorce decree was granted, she "sat home alone and
bawled." Although her decision was correct—she has never
doubted the need for the divorce—she regretted having to make
a decision. She did not want a divorce, rather she needed a
divorce. For this reason her emotion at the time of decision and
of implementation was predominantly sorrow. Had her relationship deteriorated more gradually, suffocating the love and concern for her husband, extinguishing her hope slowly, holding
her to him until the relationship turned cold, she might have
experienced a sense of relief by quitting—the "large weight
lifted from my shoulders" that many quitters experience.

The emotion at the time of decision or implementation is a
result of the heights the relationship has achieved prior to the
plunge to hopelessness, the degree of deterioration of the relationship, and thus the sense of loss as compared with that of
escape. The emotion arises from the awareness of how good the
relationship was or could have been, or from the awareness of
how bad the relationship was or could have been, or both—the

classic half-empty or half-full glass. Either half full or half empty, one's emotions are related to perceptions of the past and are thus a poor indicator of the future—and hence of success.

The Case in Perspective

Rusty's two quitting stories teach two lessons. First, the time variables—the time it took to make a decision, the time it took to implement the decision, and the time during which her relationship was a satisfactory one—are not related to success in quitting. Rusty's first divorce came after a short span of happiness and a lengthy unhappiness. The erosion was gradual but destructive. Her second marriage ended more abruptly—in a flood rather than a gradual erosion. The storm that delivered hopelessness was different. The effect was identical.

Second, her emotions at the moment of decision and when she implemented it were likewise unrelated to success. After her wearying and protracted first marriage, Rusty felt little emotion at the time of her decision to quit—only relief at the final implementation. Her second divorce, although equally necessary and as successful, caused Rusty grave sorrow. Although in both cases the future was hopeless, the histories of happiness that preceded the hopelessness were disparate. Because the outcome of Rusty's decisions was dependent upon a true vision of the future, her emotions at the time of decision and implementation, based in large part on the past, were not important to the outcome.

IT'S SO LONELY HERE TOGETHER

> Did you ever have the experience where you're on a trip and you're cruisin' along, having a high ol' time, and then it slowly dawns on you that you're on the wrong highway? That's what my marriage was all about.

Betty's first husband left her shortly after their second child was born. She was forced back to work as a nurse while trying to raise two pre-schoolers. That's when she thought she found the right highway—a wealthy dentist who wanted to marry her. He

was ten years older than Betty and recently divorced but marriage to him looked like the right direction. She called him, only
half-jokingly, the "prince."

Because this is a book about quitting, one could guess that the
prince was destined to turn into a toad, or so Betty was to perceive him.

> He helped me secure a divorce from my first husband
> and we were married. The wedding was in our new
> house, which we had designed together. It was
> magnificent—a view of the Gulf, a short walk to the
> beach, the best of everything. Overnight I was a wealthy
> woman.
>
> The problem came when I realized I loved the wealth
> and not the man who provided it. My first clue that our
> marriage wasn't so hot was when our sex life dwindled to
> about one ho-hum episode a month. He just wasn't in-
> terested, which did strange things to my self-esteem. I
> guessed he was fooling around but I wasn't about to say
> anything—I would just work on my tan or talk to the
> caterers about our next party, you know, keep busy. "You
> got a great life," I would tell myself. Once I was trying to
> cheer myself up and asked myself, "Who needs sex?" You
> can guess the answer to that one.

Betty tried. She bought new clothes and wore new demeanors
with them. Nothing changed but Betty's appearance. Finally her
husband blurted out that it pained him to see her trying to
please him; the problem was his, not hers, he confessed. He
suggested they try counseling.

The counseling encouraged Betty's husband to confide his
guilt feelings about his career and the money he pulled out of
people as a dentist. "I went into dentistry to help people," he told
her, "but most of the time I stare into a perfectly healthy mouth
and say, 'Perfectly healthy' and I get paid. Then if I have to do
something, I really make the money. Who am I helping?" And
her husband still carried guilt from all the "optional" work he
had done as a young dentist—all the pulling and filling that was
only questionably necessary.

> After months of thinking that I was helping my husband get over his guilt hangups, he suddenly confesses that for years he has quieted his inner doubts by visiting prostitutes. It turns out he was doing the dentistry for half the hookers in Florida—and he was returning the patronage. And here I thought his sex drive had dried up.

Even after this revelation, Betty could not make a decision.

> I was living in luxury with a pleasant man who wanted me to stay with him. I still had two children to think about. The kids were in the best private school and I was so comfortable.
>
> I told everything to my best friend and she told me to stay right where I was. She suggested I have affairs and even wanted to come along to singles' bars so we could both get picked up. She told me to let myself go and just think of my marriage as a wonderful job. I told her *I* couldn't do that, that I'd feel like one of his hookers. She said, "But you never have sex."

It was not an easy choice, especially when the alternative was to raise two children on her own. Betty hesitated—for two more years. Finally, sitting alone one day she screamed. Her dammed emotions had burst through.

Although quite aware of her marital shortcomings and even of her failure to rectify her problems, Betty had not experienced hopelessness before. The advice of her friends and counselor were wind in her face; her momentum to decision had been slowed. "Not a bad life," she would constantly remind herself. Then came a startling insight. Betty girded on those mighty weapons of truth—pen and paper—took time to reflect, and then wrote these words: "If I stay married, I will never experience finding someone I can truly love. I've buried myself in security."

Hopeless. A relationship that must be allowed to die so that another, more beautiful and healthy, may be born.

Suddenly what Betty had to do became obvious: first, avoid the advice of her friends and her counselor; second, consult her Self-interest.

Betty set a deadline for her decision. She would end her marriage on her birthday, three months hence, unless things improved substantially. They did not. On the morning of her birthday, Betty awoke feeling refreshed and more alive than she had felt in years. She announced her decision to seek a divorce and instructed her husband to go ahead to a dental convention out of town, as planned, while she stayed behind to begin the arrangements. He did and she did. They were divorced with rather little animosity or other emotion, for Betty desired a compromise and was ready to bear the burden of her decision.

She occasionally misses her old house, but never her husband.

The Case in Perspective

"I've buried myself . . ." That was the sound of Betty seeing Forever. She recognized the limitations of her future and accepted the hopelessness of her security. She asserted her Self-interest and laid out a plan, which was to culminate in her Clean Decision. The advice she finally ignored was typical myth-talk, mere reassurance. Her implementation was rather abrupt but nonetheless effective. Setting a deadline for a decision was arbitrary and artificial and played no significant role in her decision. The length of time taken for her decision and the implementation was based on her reluctance to forego her substantial material comfort rather than upon genuine hope for her relationship; thus, the time variables were not related to the success of her decision. Her reluctance to decide and her delayed implementation did explain her positive emotions on the day of her decision and on the day of her implementation, but these feelings were indicative of her protracted journey rather than her destination.

THE PROGRAM

Bryan is *her* name, as if she were born to challenge the man's world of a major trucking company. The parents who named her, survivors of the Great Depression, had imbued her not with assertiveness, but with a respect for security, urging her to find work with a large, stable company and to build seniority.

I just followed the program. My parents had always been company people. They worked their whole lives for a pension. Their program was: You go to work for a big company, you stay there forty years, you expect periods of unhappiness, you learn to overlook problems, you get that pension.

Bryan's program was selling trucking service—pursuing and getting orders from industrial clients for transporting their materials and merchandise. Being bright, loquacious, and different—and a woman—Bryan was quite successful.

You know when you're better than most. Your accounts do better, the compliments flow in, the errors are rare, you're well above quota, you win little pewter cups saying you had the most sales.

But all was not well with Bryan's job. She went five years without a promotion. Part of her "program" was patience, but Bryan was ambitious and Bryan was suspicious: She began to notice that in the oral history of the company she encountered but one instance of a woman being promoted to a management position—the lowest of the management positions, at that.

After five years with the company I first started feeling around for a promotion. This increased the flow of compliments I received: "We're proud of you." "You're good at your work." I wanted to threaten to resign if I wasn't promoted, but I had a child and I was not married and I was afraid. I felt I was taken advantage of because of my position. I felt trapped.

Over the course of five more trapped years, Bryan grew away from the company. She had always borne the brunt of tasteless jokes about being a woman; she had played along, diffident toward her company and its manifestation—her supervisors—in her life. Until one day. She had simply had enough.

There was an aura of intimidation. There was gossip and politics and paranoia. One man used to tell me that top management was out to get me, but that he was on my side. He said to me, "We have to stick together, because management is out to get us." He was terrified. He had me to his home for dinner, and his wife said to me, "Now, you know they're out to get Joe, and if they call you into the office to question you, what are you going to say?"

That paranoia had me wondering if anything was worth that much. We were constantly being warned of impending cutbacks in the staff and thus were being told that we should outdo our peers because we were in danger of being laid off. That atmosphere served to keep us workers quiet. It kept me from complaining about not being promoted and it forced me to put up with all the chauvinism. But one day my supervisor yelled at me, "Hey, Dummy," which is something he often called the women in the office, and I ignored him. Then he yelled, "Hey, broad," and I turned around and said, "I am not a broad, and my name is not Dummy. My name is Bryan, and I would appreciate being called Bryan."

One small step by a woman. One giant fall in company standing. In the rigid world of major corporations, overt anger is only directed *down* the table of organization. Bryan had her Realization that she would never be content to work at the trucking company but noticed it only when she allowed the resentment to escape on "My name is not Dummy" day. She had already recognized the improbability of being promoted; that day she acknowledged the impossibility.

What I did caused a lot of anger in the office. Without a doubt I was going to be standing on the other side of the fence from then on. It's hard for someone who hasn't worked in that kind of hostile work environment to understand that a little comment like that could make a lasting difference, but because I didn't go around apologizing to everyone that heard my remark or didn't wear a dunce cap and a sign that said "Call me Dummy," I was considered a drag on the office. "Watch what you say around Bryan. She's touchy."

Bryan had decided that her future included quitting but could not make that future happen in the present. She decided to quit, but could not turn her decision into reality, for she feared the financial hardship that would come with resigning her well-paying job. Also, Bryan was concerned about the effect her quitting might have on her boyfriend, whom she was planning to marry.

> I began working to save up a little nest egg to see me through after I quit, when I all of a sudden decided I just didn't need to wait any longer. I thought, "What if my guy decides to run out on me? I need his financial and emotional aid." And I just told myself, "So be it. If the relationship won't take some strain, it shouldn't be. And if it goes, I don't know what I'll do, but I'll do. Just because I don't know the answer doesn't mean the answer isn't out there." What I was saying to myself is that I was not happy and I knew that I had to do something, even if it meant a little hardship.

When a person loses hope, he often finds courage—the courage of the cornered. Nothing to lose. Might as well try. Bryan had made a Clean Decision when she asserted her Self-interest and "all of a sudden didn't need to wait." She was overcome with a sense of peace, of resignation, in quitting. But she also felt bold, even brave. She decided on a confrontation rather than a simple letter of resignation.

> I had talked with my supervisor several times during my last year about why I hadn't been promoted. His response had been to rely on some upcoming changes in the organizational structure of the whole company, to stall. This time I went in and demanded to see my personnel file—a real, real taboo. My supervisor said he would think about it. I told him I would be back in the morning for his answer.
> The next morning I was given my personnel file. I then demanded a copy of everything in the file. He turned pale and told me to come back the next morning. When I did,

I discovered that pages were missing in my copy. And there were criticisms of me that I had never been told about. I told my supervisor that there were a lot of things about my file that did not add up.

That night I cleaned out my desk, for I knew I wouldn't last long. The next day I knew something was going to happen, because the secretary was in and out of the manager's door a hundred times, looking very important, and all the managers were meeting in secret. People were asking me if I knew what was going on. Ten minutes before five my supervisor called me in and said, "I really hate to have to do this, but we are going to have to let you go. You're fired." I told him, "Never again will anyone buy my self-respect for a paycheck." That was it. I went to EEOC and filed a discrimination suit, and now the company has promoted three women into positions once reserved for men.

Bryan left that day feeling very angry, and that feeling lingered. Bryan did get married and has returned to school, preparing for a career in law. She is convinced that leaving her trucking company position was the seminal positive step of her life.

The Case in Perspective

Bryan's was a straight quitting success story: She began to lose hope in her future at the trucking company, finally had her Realization and accepted hopelessness, asserted her Self-interest, and made a Clean Decision to quit.

Other components of quitting were operating, but none were important to her success:

- Bryan did not seek the advice of others. She knew that her parents would have only instructed her to stay, and her co-workers were, by definition, those who had not quit.

- Bryan's implementation was tough and contentious, but she was successful nonetheless

- The creeping tempo of Bryan's progress through the stages of her quit (her slow disillusionment, her reluctance to decide, and her hesitation before her implementation) were a result of her security-minded background and her own unfavorable economic position rather than an indication of her future, her eventual success.

- Her feelings (mostly favorable, mostly relief) on the day of her decision were a result of her agonizingly long decision process—an end to the mental grinding toward a decision is always a good feeling—whereas the nature of her implementation (itself not related to success) was the root of her anger at the time of her departure.

GOD, SAVE ME FROM THE GODLY

You want to know what it's really like to be a minister?

The question came out angry. Peter was no longer a minister, but the swelling voice and the broad gestures remained. So did the hurt around the eyes.

I'll tell you what it's like. The pay? The pay is lousy—men of God aren't to be tempted by Mammon, so it's a constant, very private worry. The hours? The hours are the worst. Any crisis day or night and there you are. The congregation believes that you are to think first and foremost of them and that they have you always on call. If you wonder why ministers so want to increase the size of their congregations, it isn't mainly to save souls. You don't save souls by pulling in crowds from the church down the street, and that's where most of the new people would come from. It's so that you can build a staff and become the senior minister, who doesn't have to go out on every call and be at every function. A bigger church provides more money and more freedom. And more flexibility to do a job well—that's important too. A minister doesn't just have all the concerns of the congregation. There is the steady, unblinking stare of the Almighty. Ministers have the pressures of guilt as well. But even worse than the hours and the pay are the egos one must suffer. Every guy who's been a member for a few years and given a few dollars and hours thinks that his opinions of the service and the facilities are crucial. And the minister must be above reproach. A couple of beers at a pizza parlor can raise eyebrows. A sermon for peace can lose you members. A sermon for war can lose members. You can't talk about anything but ethereal matters. Or self-help, how-to-live is very popular—Pray to baby Jesus and make a million in your spare time.

Peter was the pastor of a middle-sized (one assistant, one secretary) Protestant church in the San Francisco area for sixteen years. The job was not all bad.

Oh, the joys of the job. To help a family whose son had been critically injured. To prevent a suicide. To preside at a wedding of two beautiful young people. To flail away in the pulpit with a large audience. The volley ball with the kids. The births. To drop into bed knowing you had worked to exhaustion for your Lord.

From the mountaintop to the valley of despair, Peter hung onto his life as it followed its erratic pattern of satisfactions and heartbreaks. Some days he hated to go to work—the typical worker. Some days he bounded from bed, eager for the challenge—a feeling not all men knew, Peter realized.

What made the job right, what made up for all the problems, was my conviction that no other job would do for me: I was made to serve God. God walked with me, whether he knew it or not. He spoke to me—no, not voices in the night, but I believed that I knew his will.

Then there was death. I was there so often when a child died or when a man was struck down just before he achieved his life goal. I lost my belief in Hell. It just seemed so un-Christian. Rejecting Hell, I had to *force* myself to still believe in Heaven. After a time I avoided funerals as well as I could. That was my first concession to myself that all was not as it should be.

About the time Peter was struggling with his understanding of death, his family began to disintegrate. His daughter disappeared. She was sixteen, born while Peter was still in seminary. She ran off with a garage mechanic not much older than she was.

Here was this eighteen-year-old kid, a drifter, really, a lapsed Catholic, who took my daughter away from me. She preferred him to her home and her school. I discovered how little I knew her. And it was too late. I tried to know her then, but it was too late. She had entered into a phase of deep resentment, and my attentions were not welcomed. My wife blamed me. I blamed me. I vowed not to let the same thing happen to our younger daughter.

Peter, a city boy whose face had never known a tan and whose legs had never known Levis, decided to buy a small inactive ranch. He got horses, chickens, even goats, and raised his own vegetables.

I liked it. I bought myself a Stetson and swaggered around my land. The horses bothered me a little, and the flies were a problem part of the year, but I found genuine peace when working the soil. The problem was that I was an hour's drive from the church. Some of the congregation resented that. And I had to acknowledge the resentment some felt toward my material success. The ranch was purchased with an inheritance from my folks and was more than most of the congregation that supported me could have afforded. I got closer to my family but farther from my congregation. I saw no resolution to the dilemma. And, as I got to know my wife all over again, I saw that we were not really the couple I had thought. I believe that she loved someone else, and she confessed to an affair, if not to the love. This had been her reaction to my absence, and it struck me as perfectly reasonable.

Psychologically, Peter's shoulders were not only broad but available; he accepted responsibility for his daughter's disaffection and for his wife's affair. When his church began to show the effects of his decreased involvement and attendance began to decline, he faulted himself. His world was crumbling. He tried harder, slept less, was sick more often. Renewed effort had no effect, however, except to tire him, reducing the distance to the end of his patience.

> I was trying to hold together my family and the ranch and my church while trying to sort out my own philosophical doubts. I needed six months alone, six months with my family, six months away from my family. I worried about my options but did nothing.

Peter had realized his familiar shortcomings when his daughter ran away and again when his wife confessed to an affair; he recognized his own work problems when funerals became too painful to perform. His eyes were open to his problems but not to his future. One day his assistant handed him his future.

> In order to make the church more growth-oriented, I had initiated a detailed record-keeping procedure, updated monthly, analyzed quarterly, a kind of performance check on the church and on me. I had a graph on which the attendance, membership and offerings were depicted. I hadn't looked at the records for a few months, had asked my assistant not to concern me with them. He finally decided that he had to concern me and went so far as to write a little memo showing that if present trends continued, we would have negative attendance within three years. He was trying to jolt me, because he could see that my spark was missing. He did. That night I had a long talk with my wife. She told me that if I went back to my old schedule and moved them back into the city, she would leave me. Then she told me that she was thinking of leaving me anyhow. I asked her for six months more before she did anything. She agreed.

Peter's future gave *him* a hard stare: recommit his energies to the church and lose his family; devote his energies to his family and watch his church decline. Defeat or failure. The noose or the chair. Being a man of God and a man of reason, Peter explored compromises. Another assistant pastor? The chairman of the budget committee confided that the budget was in deep trouble and that the rumors about Peter were getting nasty. A different church? The daughter still at home was in high school and demanded that she be allowed to finish in the same school, and his wife refused to move.

> As I matured in my Christianity, I had stopped making bargains with God—I never could get him to shake on a deal—but in my prayers I asked God for his inspiration. I needed a miracle, and I told him that if one didn't arrive within three months, I was going to leave the ministry for some material pursuit such as buying a Burger King franchise or becoming a stockbroker. It wasn't a threat, because I knew that he'd get along fine without me in the church.
>
> The problem with miracles these days is that they are so hard to spot. My daughter finally broke off with the mechanic. A wealthy widow left money to the church. Were these signs? I didn't know these to be miracles any more than the arrival of an offer to teach in a nearby college or finally learning to ride a horse.
>
> One night, as my wife's deadline for possibly leaving approached, I rode my horse out into the hills and sat alone watching the evening sky. Sitting there, I decided to approach my decision completely selfishly. I forgot what God might think or my regional minister or my wife or the congregation. Just me. When I was honest with myself, I found that the congregation was getting on my nerves, and that was reflected in my work. I was stale. I wanted very much to have the last few years of the nuclear family together in one household. I wanted to ranch. I wanted to come home at night and feel good about my work without wondering what or who I had forgotten or offended.
>
> Once I was honest, it was an easy decision. And a correct decision for everyone involved. Who was I kidding?

The church would collapse without me? With me it might collapse. I knew that it was better to bow out than to be pushed out; that way I would still have an option of returning. And if I didn't make the effort to unite my family, I would always blame myself. So I thanked God for not interfering in my life with any of his miracles and I wrote out a tear-stained letter of resignation.

Peter confessed to taking just a little un-Christian delight in seeing a "young star" of a minister having difficulties uniting his old congregation. He also expressed a Christian delight in having established a healthy relationship with his wife and at least one of his daughters. His new teaching career is "challenging but not burdensome." He believes that his resignation from the ministry has lessened the demands on his philosophy and thus bolstered his faith.

The Case in Perspective

Again in this case the quitting decision was protracted; the hopelessness came slowly to a man of hope. A deadline imposed by his wife forced Peter to examine his underdeveloped Self-interest and make a Clean Decision.

The presence of a deadline for a decision is not related to the success of the quitting decision, not because deadlines have no effect but because the effect is unpredictable. In two previous cases a deadline forced a decision prior to the Clean Decision—the teacher who faced contract renewal during a time of vacillation about whether to remain in teaching and the man who called off his wedding in a time of extreme uncertainty about his future: Both decisions were largely incorrect. In the case of Peter, the deadline was the impetus to overcome a stalled decision process. When a deadline makes the components of success clear, the deadline is, of course, a valuable tool. But when it forces a decision before things have built up to the Clean Decision, the deadline makes the outcome uncertain.

THE SIX COMPONENTS IN PERSPECTIVE

The six "silent" variables—those without a consistent relationship to success—are:

1. Smooth time. The length of time the relationship was running successfully is normally a factor in the length of time taken to make a decision to quit, but is not related to the success of that decision. Once the relationship has become untenable, its history is irrelevant: The outcome of a war is not decided by the number of preceding years of peace.

2. Time for decision. The time taken to reach a decision is not related to success. The final score, not the number of time outs, will be remembered.

3. Time to implement. The implementation of the decision to quit, especially the Clean Break, is not important to the eventual success of the decision. The road chosen, not the vehicle, decides the destination.

4. Presence of deadlines for decision. Deadlines can push the reluctant to success or can rush the undecided into a premature decision; thus, the presence of deadlines has no consistent pattern with successful quitting. Greater speed into one of life's turns is advantageous—unless the turn is missed.

5 and 6. Feelings on the day of decision and implementation. The extent of positive or negative emotions at the time of decision is related to the length of time for the decision, the state of the relationship, and whether the quitter anticipates resistance. Thus the emotions are the result of components that themselves are not positively correlated to success. Likewise, the emotional state on the day of implementation is principally determined by how much the relationship has deteriorated. The long-suffering person welcomes death. The unconscious do not welcome consciousness. The emotions of quitting are determined largely by the past; success is in the future.

APPENDIX

THE DAUTEN MODEL

QUITTING is to a relationship what the black capsule is to a secret agent—not pleasant to contemplate, not pleasant to employ, but preferable to the alternative. But the quitter can be assured of something the secret agent cannot: an afterlife. When the quitter has lived the four stages of successful quitting, the life after quitting is rather certain to be an improvement. The path to a successful quit was plotted in chapters 2 through 5 and is pictured below.

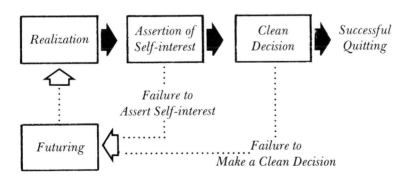

The Dauten Model

The quitting model can be addressed mathematically as well as schematically. The mathematical expression is more precise and permits some subtle differences to show between general quitting decisions and the more limited genre of career quits. Converting the statistical jargon of mathematical modeling* into a simple scoring system:

Each of the four variables (Futuring, Realization, Self-interest, and Clean Decision) are given scores from 0 to 10, where 10 is the strongest possible presence of the variable.

Success is given a score from 1 to 10, where 10 is total success (rapid adjustment, no regrets, and complete willingness to repeat the decision).

$$3(Futuring) + 3(Realization) + 2(Self\text{-}interest) + 2(Clean\ Decision) = Success\ Score$$

In words, the intensity of the Futuring variable was given a score ranging from 0 to 10, which is multiplied by 3. That result is then ready to be added to the multiplied score of the other three variables. Once the four variables have been multiplied by their respective weights and added together, an estimated score for success is produced, ranging from 0 to 100. As an example, if a given individual had a strong sense of the future (scored a 9), a fairly strong Realization (scored a 7), clearly asserted Self-interest (scored a 10), and finally, had made a very Clean Decision (also scored a 10), the formula would suggest a success score of 88:

$$3(9) + 3(7) + 2(10) + 2(10) = 88$$

The success score of 88 is very high and is associated with a very rapid adjustment, few regrets, and a clear willingness to repeat the decision. The 100-point scale is arbitrary, selected for convenience; it was, however, defined so that any success score of 60 or greater is associated with the clear indication of the

*A step-wise multiple regression was run. In order to simplify the result, a multiple regression was then run on the four variables that emerged as most important to describing success. The R-squared was just over .8.

quitter having made the "correct" decision. Scores below 60 but 40 or higher were cases where the adjustment was slow and painful or the decision had not been totally accepted by the individual but nonetheless seemed "correct." Only the scores below 40 were "incorrect" decisions to quit.

A separate formula was developed for career-quitting decisions. Only slightly different than the scoring for quits in general, it is

$$3.5(Futuring) + 3(Realization) + 2(Self\text{-}interest)$$
$$+ 1.5(Clean\ Decision) = Success\ Score$$

In the case of careers the Clean Decision becomes slightly less important, whereas Futuring becomes slightly more important, reflecting the greater role of rational contemplation and the lesser need for the subconscious/emotional commitment of the Clean Decision.

In both the general and the career model, the majority of the 100 points possible come from the Futuring and Realization components. This suggests the leading role played by hopelessness in the quitting decision. Once a state of hopelessness has been reached, Self-interest and a Clean Decision serve to allow the person to act: Futuring and the Realization are seeing and believing, while Self-interest and the Clean Decision are acting.

THE DAUTEN MODEL IN PERSPECTIVE

One critical reason for the existence of the book you hold is the previous absence of a thorough analysis of human behavior in leaving an important relationship; however, some previous, related research has been undertaken and should be reviewed briefly to place the Dauten model in perspective.

The most practical related study was undertaken by the United Church of Christ to try better to understand individuals who had quit a position as a church pastor. When the ex-pastors were asked how their self-image had changed since resigning, over half of those having an opinion reported a positive change, and less than one-fourth reported a negative change (the remainder felt that their self-image was unchanged). When asked if they were interested in returning to a pastor's position, approximately 10 percent said that they were "eager" to do so, another 10 percent felt that a return to a pastorate would make them "equally as happy" as they are in their present position, while the remainder—the majority—preferred not to return.

Thus the findings among the sample of ministers suggested the same general conclusion as the interviews for this book: The large majority of those who do quit believe that quitting was a positive, correct decision.

Although little, if any, academic investigation of quitting has been undertaken, a large, indeed corpulent, body of research on decision making exists. The authors of a recent book entitled *Decision Making* were kind enough to summarize the "extensive literature on effective decision making" as follows:

> The decision maker, to the best of his ability and within his information-processing capabilities

1. thoroughly canvasses a wide range of alternative courses of action

2. surveys the full range of objectives to be fulfilled and the values implicated by the choice

3. carefully weighs whatever he knows about the costs and risks of negative consequences, as well as the positive consequences, that could flow from each alternative

4. intensively searches for new information relevant to further evaluation of the alternatives

5. correctly assimilates and takes account of any new information or expert judgment to which he is exposed, even when the information or judgment does not support the course of action he initially prefers

6. reexamines the positive and negative consequences of all known alternatives, including those originally regarded as unacceptable, before making a final choice

7. makes detailed provisions for implementing or executing the chosen course of action, with special attention

to contingency plans that might be required if various
known risks were to materialize

Thus all of the literature on "effective decision making" can be
reduced to: Look before you cross the street. The academic
solution is sufficiently broad to analyze everything, and thus
nothing.

The authors of *Decision Making*, I. L. Janis and Leon Mann,
did, however, undertake experiments with procedures designed
to reduce the risk in personal decision making. Their first suggestion, "decision counseling," seems rather weak in the light of
the findings of this research. But two other suggestions do correspond to identified techniques utilized by successful quitters.
The first of these is the "pro and con" balance sheet—the magic
of pen and paper. (In an experiment involving college students'
decisions on dieting or on choosing a college, the use of the
balance sheet "showed a substantial reduction in postdecisional
regret." Amen.) The second technique is a procedure for Futuring called psychodrama. The individual is to project himself into
the future and speak of what happened to him since the decision. No experimental results are available, but this technique,
performed internally rather than before a class or a counselor,
was common to successful quitters. A final suggestion offered by
Janis and Mann is "emotional inoculation for postdecisional setbacks"; the individual is encouraged to envision all the problems
to be encountered—anticipation should thus lessen the impact
of "negative consequences." Although the nature of the implementation was found not to be related to successful quitting,
such emotional inoculation might have a short-term ameliorat-
ing effect and thus could be useful.

What the literature on decision making assumes, of course, is
an individual who is consciously facing a decision. Such an assumption disregards the most important aspect of the quitting
decision—arriving at the decision point. Futuring and the
Realization—hopelessness—are the archetypal prerequisites to
meaningful contemplation of quitting. The literature on decision making thus tends to ignore the process of recognizing the
need for decision, a process that, in effect, tends to make the

decision. Having reached hopelessness and thus the need for a quitting decision, the correct choice is often made clear.

In human relations, the process of making choices clear is perhaps more difficult and more important than are the decision criteria for the choice. Once clear, the decisions tend to be rather easy. The determination to act upon the choice is difficult, requiring the impetus of the assertion of Self-interest and a Clean Decision. Academic decision-making models emphasize choosing: the Dauten model for quitting emphasizes (1) the recognition of the need for a decision; and (2) the determination to act.

INDEX